_____*More*

_____*Devotions*

_____*for*

_____*Families*

_____*That*

_____*Can't*

_____*Sit*

_____*Still*

MORE DEVOTIONS FOR FAMILIES

That Can't Sit Still

CAROLYN WILLIFORD

VICTOR BOOKS®

A DIVISION OF SCRIPTURE PRESS PUBLICATIONS INC.
USA CANADA ENGLAND

Unless otherwise noted, all references are from the *Holy Bible, New International Version,* © 1973, 1978, 1984, International Bible Society. Used by permission of Zondervan Bible Publishers.

Library of Congress Cataloging-in-Publication Data

Williford, Carolyn.
 More devotions for families that can't sit still/Carolyn Williford.
  p. cm.
 Includes bibliographical references and index.
 ISBN 0-89693-252-4
 1. Family—Prayer-books and devotions, etc.—English. I. Title.
BV255.W492 1991
249—dc20   91-13922
                                                                   CIP

1 2 3 4 5 6 7 8 9 10 Printing/Year 95 94 93 92 91

With appreciation and love,
this book is dedicated to

Carol
Donna
Tim

and so many others who have lovingly befriended
Robb and Jay.
Thanks for investing your lives in my sons.

This has been our summer for "major appliance breakdown." I should have known great things were coming early in June when I reached for the automatic ice cube tray and was immediately drenched with water—*not* ice. After the initial shock wore off, major panic set in as I frantically checked the other contents of the freezer. Yes, everything had thawed and of course the warranty had long ago expired. But even though most appliances do seem to wait until just after the warranty expires to go on the fritz, I *like* warranties. I feel secure knowing that, no matter what goes wrong, my guarantee will give me what I paid for and desire.

However, when my sons were born, they did not come with *any* guarantees. Period. As parents we put enormous time, effort, expense (emotional and physical being far greater than monetary expense), and—how can I put it?—part of our very selves into our children. But nowhere can we find or claim to have a receipt that succinctly states: "Because of your effort and investment, this child comes with a written guarantee. He or she will, at the age of eighteen, make only correct major life decisions and forever live a godly life." But we parents of school-age kids don't quite accept the idea of no-guarantee parenting. Instead, our age seems especially susceptible to searching for the right *formula* for parenthood. We think that—hope and pray that—if we strive to do everything just right, everything possible for our children, then we'll click into this magic formula, and we *will* indeed find a type of guarantee. But unfortunately, this guarantee does *not* exist. But, oh, how I wish it did!

Does that mean we parents should stop working, stop trying to teach our children what the essence of life is all about—thirsting after Jesus Christ? Absolutely not! Instead, we need to spend less energy in searching for that magic formula and focus more on just *what* we're investing in, what has eternal value. We parents need to put our time and effort into unquestionably demonstrating just where we place value—in our children. And to whom is this demonstration directed? To *God.* To our *children.*

This motivation was what pushed me to attempt a new type of family devotions, active ones that combined worship, fellowship, and fun into a "living picture" of the Christian lifestyle. Rejecting the "sit-still-while-we-parents-read" approach because of its repetitive and boring connotations for our sons, I strove for a family worship time that graphically showed God's Word is *alive* and still so very applicable to today. We experimented, plodded, sometimes totally bombed, and yet often succeeded beyond my greatest hopes in accomplishing worthwhile family worship.

These past six years have been full of surprises (good *and* bad!), joy, and indescribable memories. In my first book, *Devotions for Families That Can't Sit Still,* we Willifords invited you to take a glimpse into our home and to share in these memories. We again gladly offer suggestions for devotions that we have used over the past two years. Some will provide you with surprises—good *and* bad!—but we are delighted to say that we *can* indeed offer you a guarantee! If your family uses each devotion in this book and then your love for God and each other has not grown, you may have your *old* relationship back!

Setting New Patterns: Getting Control of That Schedule

I've learned that getting parents excited and motivated to commit to these active devotions is *one* thing; seeing them carry out the commitment and actually *do* them is another entirely! Yes, making changes and beginning new patterns is always difficult, but this is especially true concerning today's families for probably one major reason: THE CALENDAR.

Last spring, a typical week of evening activities around the Williford home could go something like this:

TUESDAY: Jay—attending Awana; Robb—leading Awana;

Dad (and possibly Mom also) — attending church meeting
WEDNESDAY: Prayer meeting; Jay — baseball practice and/or
game; Robb — youth group band practice
THURSDAY: Robb — youth group meeting; Jay — baseball
practice and/or game; Dad — church meeting
FRIDAY: Robb — youth group activity; Jay — baseball game
SATURDAY: Robb — discipleship group; Jay — baseball game

And we could throw in assorted meetings, rehearsals, band con-
certs, school and church activities, etc. You get the idea, I'm sure,
because your calendar most likely looks just as harried. Different
activities possibly, but the point is the same: *No vacancies!*

You'll note, however, that I did not include Monday night in
this list. That's because Monday night at the Williford house has
been family night for some time now. Yes, we have last-minute
appointments, emergencies, and other meetings that sometimes
interrupt that pattern. But we're still committed to a night for *us*,
a night when we can plan a special activity to worship God
together. And that's the first step in gaining a regular night
together: GET IT ON THE CALENDAR. Written down. In ink.

But what do you do when there simply is no night available —
not even *one* when your family members can all meet together?
What if each night contains a myriad of activities, some involving
scurrying to deliver a child to one end of town and another to the
opposite? (And of course you, the parent, are supposed to be at
yet *another* destination.)

Maybe your children are still small and you can't relate to this
hectic schedule. You need to be aware of what's ahead and how
to avoid the gradual and seductive slip into this lifestyle. Those of
you who are relating to our calendar, however, first need to
evaluate just how and why this hurry-up pace came about before
we can even begin to identify, control, and cure it. Sound like I'm
describing a disease? Yes, I think that's *exactly* what it is, and it
can be *lethal* for your family!

The Disease: "Amusement Park" Syndrome
Not long ago I read an article in the *Chicago Tribune* about Mr.
Howard Fields, a designer of "hundreds of glitzy and glamorous

aquatic spectaculars of the era of conspicuous consumption."[1] In other words, he is an architect of swimming pools—*fabulous* swimming pools. A rectangular, normal pool is out, Mr. Fields tells us. Instead, "[People] want instant jungle. Instant ocean. You've got to give them an experience they've never had before. . . . Twenty years ago, they didn't have these expectations."[2] And concerning what we do with our available time he says, " 'See, people try to do more with their time these days. It's not just a matter of barbecue in the backyard on a redwood table. . . . When they go on vacation they want'—here Fields claps his hands loudly—'to hit it real hard.' "[3] Could it be that we parents want to "hit it real hard" in nearly every area of our lives? Especially in relation to the activities of our children?

Certainly we can note that today's parents' expectations are far beyond those of previous generations. This is the age of tremendous opportunities, computers, technology, and thus an amazing wealth of worthwhile experiences that are available for our kids—some not even thought of a few decades ago. Assuming that all these experiences are worthwhile and beneficial—swimming lessons, computer classes, baseball games, after-school enrichment programs, Boy and Girl Scouts, band, gymnastics (need I go on?)—when do we say no? When do we say enough?

When we combine Mr. Fields' philosophy (which seems essentially to be, "I want more!") with all that is available for our children to do, we parents can often feel intense pressure and even *fear* that *my children might miss out on something!* When we then allow that pressure to control us—and our lives—then I believe we have a serious disease. The "Amusement Park" Syndrome.

Possibly you need an examination for signs of the "Amusement Park" Syndrome in your family. Check your lifestyle for these deadly symptoms:

SYMPTOM ONE: Your calendar already looks like a computer printout, but still you regularly add new activities without first realistically examining how they will affect your lifestyle. Every new activity ("He can be in the school variety show this year? Great! Sign him up!") appears to be a terrific opportunity that can't be missed—and therefore is added without true evaluation. Do I have the ability to analyze and prioritize? Can I say no to a worthwhile yet time-consuming activity?

SYMPTOM TWO: Dinner is served in "shifts" regularly. Junior grabs a hot dog before soccer practice; sister bolts her peanut butter and jelly sandwich while being taxied to gymnastics; Mom eats *while* taxiing (of course!); Dad eats at "McDarrel's" on the way to son's ball game. Yes, occasional nights like this description seem to be part of the fallout of this generation's pace. But has this routine become *normal*—and therefore acceptable—at my home?

SYMPTOM THREE: Children are pushed at such a frantic pace that they show the beginning signs of stress and burnout—headaches, stomachaches, nightmares, irritability. Hard to believe? Eileen Ogintz tells us that this pressure begins now *at the preschool age.* Eager parents go to extensive means to enroll their children at the best preschools because of the "very strong don't-leave-my-kid-behind sentiment."[4] Why is this so important? Because "when they're two, they're already worried about how they'll be tracked when they go to school."[5]

Numerous educators and psychologists are studying the effects of this hurried lifestyle on our kids. In another article by Ogintz, she quotes child psychologist Antoinette Saunders who says, "People schedule family life around the activities, with the priority on the activities. . . . It's a catastrophe. We don't value time together."[6] What do our kids think about it? " 'Children tell me they feel their parents want to get rid of them by sending them to all of these activities instead of just playing with them,' says Saunders."[7] Is this the message I'm sending my kids?

SYMPTOM FOUR: Sunday becomes our only day to not rush anywhere and just be together; therefore, attending church easily becomes *expendable.* After a full week of rushing out the door for every activity imaginable, going to church as a family has become just another hassle. Have I dismissed weekly family worship at our local church to make up for my frantic lifestyle?

The flip side may also be the norm in our homes: incorporating the same harried pace into our Sunday church activities, we merely go through the paces—at top speed and with several doses of irritation thrown in. Not only does our attendance at church have no meaning, but true worship becomes an impossibility. Have Sunday activities become another set of *intrusions* that we eagerly check off as "Done!" on our calendars?

SYMPTOM FIVE: Evenings are so heavily scheduled that we do not have *one* night a week to be together—*at home!*—as a family. And on the rare occasions that we do have a night at home, we're so exhausted that our main activity is to position ourselves like zombies in front of the television. Besides, there is this wonderfully educational show on PBS.

Evaluation Time: Does My Family Have This Disease?
First we need to dispel the myth that we Christians wouldn't, *couldn't* be susceptible to this deadly virus. And I label it a virus because that seems to describe it so well: the pressure and fear that causes us to over-schedule our lives often occur because our *neighbor's* kids are in these worthwhile activities. (I'm sure you've heard it many times—"But Mom! Sally's parents are letting her sign up for skating lessons!") We are not immune to wanting the best for our children, nor should we be. But we need to be on guard for wanting a *best* that is merely a disguise for Mr. Fields' "I want more!" Carried to its extreme, wanting the *best* can lead to burned-out kids.

No, we Christian parents cannot claim to possess a fail-proof vaccination. And as a matter of fact, we have yet *another* dimension of activities to deal with. Worthwhile activities. Namely, *church* activities. As a pastor's wife, I know I'm treading on dangerous ground! But as our churches offer a wealth of activities for our children, we must keep in mind the local church's desire to provide a multitude of differing opportunities. I know that our church attempts to offer programs for all types of kids: athletic, musical (choral and instrumental), outgoing, reserved, creative, intellectual, and learning disabled kids. Does this mean then that the Christian Education Board intends for every child to be in every program? No! Instead, our church offers this vast assortment so that each child can choose the programs that fits his or her needs and wants. The families that push their children to be in *every* activity available are probably going to find themselves resenting the very programs that the church intended to *help* parents in their difficult job of raising kids.

Because Christians are not immune, our first line of defense has to be this realization; only then can we begin to take a realistic look at our lives and evaluate according to our spoken priorities. And I use the phrase *spoken priorities* because too often that is all they are—spiritual-sounding words on a list that we count off so easily. (Please understand that I'm speaking to *myself* first of all. These hard lessons—ones I'll forever be working on—come out of my own experience.) Priorities cannot merely be a passive list; instead, priorities call for an active evaluation of our everyday lives. *Am I truly living what I say I am?* And where should I begin my first evaluation? *In my home—the laboratory for spiritual growth!*

The Cure: Saying No!

I think the word *no* is terribly misleading. How can it be so small, simple-sounding, and therefore seemingly easily spoken and carried out? Toddlers defiantly spit it out countless times every day, *parents* of toddlers probably double their children's use of the word, and we who now have teenagers find we're back into that same old cycle! After so much practice, why can't we as adults use it with wisdom, discretion, confidence, and then follow through with definite action?

When our children are toddlers, the no's generally follow obvious threats to their security. "No! You may not touch a hot stove!" or, "No! You may not stand up in the grocery cart!" And we then carry out definite action because our child's safety is at stake. But saying no to a worthwhile activity such as ice skating lessons seems selfish on my part: I'm denying my child the right to a new experience that will be beneficial and fun, and most importantly, probably boost his or her self-image—an absolute *must* for today's kids. So how can I possibly say no to this activity? Or for that matter, any other new experience that comes along?

Maybe the answer lies in this understanding: I must view too many activities as a threat to my child's security and safety—a threat just like touching a hot stove or standing in a shopping cart. As parents, we are responsible for our children's security, and if we overschedule our children to the point that they're showing early signs of burnout and stress, then we *need* to say no. Or, if we do not have a family night, then we also must say no to outside activities because of the invaluable benefits provided by a family experiencing worthwhile time together—bonding, self-image boosting from family members who demonstrate "*you are a unique and needed part of this family,*" fellowship, fun, *security*.

Craig and I have—with frowns of disapproval from other parents and our own inward struggles—said no to numerous worthwhile activities for our sons. We did so only after careful evaluation of our priorities and the effects these activities would have on our schedules. Yes, we felt guilty! But later we felt relieved and thankful when we heard other parents complain about their harried lifestyles because of the opportunity that we passed up. We discovered that we didn't regret our decision. And amazingly, neither did our sons!

The Result: You Control That Schedule

Once you have summoned the courage to manage your first no, you will discover hidden benefits. The next season of the year will bring another wealth of opportunities and again you will be faced with giving that negative response. And you will struggle again with the fear, pressure, and guilt involved in your decisions. But once you have decided that a wonderful activity can be missed (and your child will not suffer irreparable damage!), you'll note that you've made the first gigantic step: you've set a precedent. And that makes the *second* no just a bit easier.

Second, and maybe for the first time, you will feel a sense of "*We're* in better control of our schedule," rather than, "Our schedule always controls us." Note that I didn't say that we'll always be in control; weeks when we rush everywhere in a hurry-scurry lifestyle are just a part of this generation, I believe. But instead of this being the norm, hopefully an out-of-control week is now abnormal. Once we've found that we can hold some reign over our activities, the more we realize that the reverse makes our calendars a relentless master that dictate to us! And this makes me all the more determined to keep evaluating, weighing, prioritizing each new opportunity that comes our way.

Lastly, we hope that your decisions will guarantee a family night inked onto your calendar—a night set aside to worship God together. You cannot begin to reach this commitment if you have not already committed to the decisions that will ultimately make this evening possible. Go ahead. Say no! You might even feel like a toddler again!

Notes

1. *Nathan Cobb, "A Geyser of Ideas,"* Chicago Tribune, *5 January 1989, sec. 5, p. 1, col. 1.*

2. *Cobb, p. 1, col. 3.*

3. *Cobb, p. 1, col. 3.*

4. *Eileen Ogintz, "Preschool Frenzy,"* Chicago Tribune, *3 April 1989, Sec. 5, p. 5, col. 5.*

5. *Ogintz, p. 5, col. 6.*

6. *Eileen Ogintz, "Kid Burnout,"* Chicago Tribune, *6 April 1989, sec. 5, p. 3, col. 1.*

7. *Ogintz, p. 3, col. 4*

One
GETTING THE MOST
FROM DEVOTIONAL TIMES

As in my first book, each one of these devotions has been used in the Williford "laboratory." They came out of my personal devotions, evident individual family member's needs, and family needs (and wants!) for that time and season of the year. (Please note that most of our family's more worshipful devotions are associated with holiday traditions; because these were listed in my first book, they are not repeated in this one. Therefore, if you desire other ideas for more reverent worship, please see a copy of my first book.) Hopefully you'll be able to use these suggestions and then springboard to tailor-made devotions for your unique family that come from your own experience and needs.

One different approach in this book as compared to the first—which obviously reflects our growing sons' ages—is the "Preteen/Teen and Parent—Developing the Intimate Relationship" section. As parents we certainly feel a constant need to help our children prepare for the teen years. Committing to a regular family devotional time is one important and beneficial way to reach this goal. But Craig and I also wanted to give each of our sons one-on-one time and attention for these very crucial years. Therefore, we instituted a number of traditional activities to do with each one—individually. Because these have been helpful to us as parents and to our sons, we offer these as suggestions for your preteens and teens too.

Capturing Interest
Whenever I have presented this material, parents generally ask me these two basic questions: "We've never done anything like

this before, so how do we get started?" and "Once we've begun, how do we keep our kids interested?"

Beginning can be tricky—your kids may think you've complete-ly lost your sanity if you start with something like "Proverbs: Carrying Excess Baggage"—in which family members are to carry around a brick all day! However, I would begin with something very active and fun like "Winter Blahs: 'Presto-Changeo' " or "Crazy Balloon Bible Drill Relay." (From my first book, friends have used "Killing Giants" as an introductory devotion.) This first active family worship should whet your family's appetite for what's to come. You definitely want to make an initial statement that this will indeed be different, active, fun, and beneficial to the family. Once everyone has caught on—which in our home means "heaven knows what Mom has planned for us *this* week!"—then I think you'll find your family responding flexibly to more serious worship times, active Bible story and concept combinations, and just plain fun.

I've noticed that I use Larry Richard's "hook" idea from his "hook, book, look, took" formula in *Creative Bible Teaching.*[1] Almost always I construct a "table marker," 3" x 5" file cards that I tape together to put on the table at supper. (Specific instructions for the table marker are given later.) This table marker generally provides the "hook" or attention getter for our devotions that evening. Not long ago I wrote "Developing Whiskers!" on the table marker and kept everyone guessing—incorrectly!—about what we were going to do. Another time I wrote out Proverbs 25:15-22. After telling my family that we were going to scientifical-ly demonstrate *one* of the Proverbs, I kept them puzzling (and laughing!) over which one of those we were about to do also. (You might want to look up this reference to appreciate the joke!) The point is to keep them guessing by throwing out attractive "lures"; these hints and bits of information then are used to reel in their attention.

Keeping Interest

We parents also need an essential element: the ability to be active participants, sometimes exhibiting a childlike attitude. In an arti-cle by David C. Rudd, he quotes rabbis who told a class of adults that "some play-acting, a touch of 'child-like' behavior and loads of creativity will help liven up the traditional [*seder*] meal and make it more meaningful."[2] Later he quotes Rabbi Poupko, who says, "I had a grandfather who was a great rabbi. . . . You know what he used to do at the seder? He used to get up and march around the table with a matzo in a sack like a hobo to demonstrate to everyone there how the Jews left Egypt."[3] Rudd says the class responded with giggles, but Poupko continued, "I'm dead serious. . . . That's what you're asked to do . . . behave like a child."[4] Exactly!

Yes, I suppose Craig and I have looked just plain ridiculous running through the house (tied to Robb or Jay, by the way), feeding each other ice cream bars (and of course getting chocolate and ice cream all over our faces in the process), bopping each other with empty wrapping paper tubes and playing croquet indoors with kitchen utensils. Do we care? Not one bit! Instead, we enter into this kind of fun joyfully, knowing that it brings glory to God in so many ways! And when we as parents lead the way with this type of pattern, generally our kids will follow suit, grinning (though maybe skeptically at first!) all the way.

Be sure to alternate your devotional offerings too. I usually follow a more serious worship time with a very active "just plain fun" the next week. The key is to be *flexible,* being sensitive to what your family needs *this week.* This may also mean a change in plans *today* if children are too excited for a serious worship or if a child needs a last-minute self-image builder because of a recent emotional wound.

Sometimes you may need an open forum—a time to talk out a family dispute or problem. At these times we start with a devotion we've entitled, "How Do I Feel When. . . ?" Our family uses this often (many times at our sons' request), and we have found it to be immensely helpful for our communication. And again, flexibility to need is paramount. If I've planned another devotion but find that we need to communicate on an important topic, I tuck away the other devotion for later.

Most importantly, make sure your family worship fits *you* and the unique and special family that you are. Prayerfully seeking your family's needs (together and individually) is a prerequisite for beginning and continuing worthwhile family devotions.

Adapting Devotions for Age Differences

Though this section may be repetitious to those of you who read my first book, I again offer these helps for others who need assistance in knowing what is appropriate for a child's age. The devotions in this book are applicable for the elementary and junior high years, ages six through thirteen. However, our sons are now at the upper end of this spectrum (and beyond!) since they are now twelve and fifteen years old. Because the devotions are so adaptable, however, most can be stretched for these younger and older age groups. And I have good news to report: after over six years of this format and charging full steam into the teen years, our sons still enthusiastically look forward to and join in these active family devotions.

An appropriate time to begin this type of format would be when a child is about six years old. In our experience, this was the age at which our children became bored with the repetitive reading-and-singing family worship that we had always done together. School introduces experiences which help children grow in a number of areas: cooperation in group activities, fine motor coordination for handling crayons and pencils, gross motor coordination for various active games, and working with language, reading, and writing. These various skills are important to this type of family devotion. When adapting these for children from ages six to thirteen, parents must ask themselves some important questions about their children's attention spans and abilities.

First, ask yourself, *How long is my child's attention span?* In other words, how long can he or she sit, listen, and learn? If you have two, three, or more children, how will you adjust times? Obviously, young children just cannot pay attention or absorb as much as the older child. Important clue: look for the signs. When children begin wiggling more than they are listening, poking little brother, or asking what's for dinner tomorrow, time is up. Remember that *mood* is also to be taken into account. When our sons reach the "perpetual giggle" stage, they are past the point of educational benefit. (We have also learned that's when we find out how much patience Mom and Dad possess.)

Next ask, *What abilities by ages do my children demonstrate?* Knowing and understanding age-related abilities can be helpful in planning devotions for our families, so I offer the following information for a guide.

Ages five–seven—Children at this stage of development have a limited understanding of time; thus, the promise of a trip to the beach next year means little to a five-year-old. He can't grasp the concept of "next year." They also cannot understand concepts or application of illustrations. To talk to a child in this age category about motivations (from "Motivations: Getting to the Heart of Them") would just be confusing. But memorizing Scripture (preferably easy ones, but sometimes even ones which they cannot yet fully comprehend), acting out Bible stories in charades or skits, or making a family banner *are* activities within their abilities. Children of this age need to focus on one thing at a time (thus repetition—in various styles and using different tools is helpful); they're self-centered (did we parents need to be told *that?*); and they're very curious—a great quality for teachability.

Ages seven–eleven—Somewhere in this age range children begin to conceptualize, and this is when the possibilities for application really begin. And what possibilities! We can use our creative energy to visualize as we take children from the specific to the general. A cocoon can provide a wonderful illustration of how to help children apply concepts. By demonstrating a *normal* cocoon and a *helped* cocoon (helping the moth causes it to die), we illustrate—visually and graphically—how and why God chooses not to do the maturing process *for* His children. Strength comes through struggle. Also, remember that children within these ages need organized, concrete, and literal illustrations to teach generalizations. That's why advanced preparation is so important and visual aids of all varieties are helpful. Repeat these applications in many ways to insure that they do grasp the concept being taught.

Most of these devotions can be adapted for younger or older

children, depending on a family's needs. Even "How Do I Feel When. . . ?" can be done by children who cannot yet write. Our children drew pictures that represented their feelings (as did Mom and Dad); now that we're long past the need for drawing, our sons still insist on an illustration. It seems that they view the drawing as a major part of the fun. (If you have an older toddler, put him or her in a high chair with a crayon to create a "lovely" picture too.)

Please feel free to adapt, stretch, or use these devotions as a springboard to create your own times together. Just as we are a unique and God-designed family, so is your family. Our prayer is that these devotions will bring out the specialness with which you have been blessed.

Basic Instructions

Though many of the devotions in this book do not fit any general pattern, most do follow a common progression. This order developed in part because of our concern for quality educational experiences and also because of children's inherent enjoyment of repetitive patterns. Our sons feel comfortable with and like this order. Part of their enthusiasm seems to be their anticipation of the expected fun! The basic pattern we follow is this:

1. *Short prayer first*—Beginning with a long prayer or asking for prayer requests at this time just doesn't work for us. The kids are generally too keyed up for concentration or concern for others to have a quality time in prayer. Thus, we share only a short prayer at the beginning, asking God to direct our time together.

2. *Bible reading*—This comes next because their ability to sit still and listen for details is the highest at this time. (Please note that the opening prayer has set an atmosphere of "It's time to settle down now.") Any major points that we want to impress on them are made here, for later they'll be much too wiggly to absorb the heavier information.

3. *Activities*—Saving the most exciting activities for last is always a must. We have found that once the boys are in high gear, there is virtually no way for them to return to a calm

instructional type of teaching (except for discipline measures, which we try to avoid at all costs during our devotions). It is really unfair to expect this of children; they just can't switch gears as quickly as adults.

4. *Closing prayer*—Though our boys may be excited from the preceding activities, they have learned to adapt to our pattern of closing prayer. Focusing on spiritual principles during the devotion seems to have made an impression concerning the importance of prayer. Yes, sometimes we do find that we must cut this time shorter than we would like because they are not concentrating. Most of the time, however, their prayers reflect an understanding and personal application of what we have just learned together. We also use this time to share prayer requests and pray for each other, which is a real bonding experience for us as a family.

Materials Needed

There are several materials that I keep handy for future use in our devotions. Since I use these items constantly, keeping them in supply eliminates running to the store each week. Therefore, I suggest you begin collecting them now, and replenish supplies as you use them:

- notebook paper
- felt-tip pens (all colors, broad and fine points)
- crayons
- construction paper (all colors)
- yarn, string
- 3" x 5" file cards
- Scotch Tape and masking tape
- poster board
- cardboard
- candles
- boxes, assorted sizes
- wrapping paper, ribbon
- balloons
- felt
- assorted "junk"—wrapping paper tubes, surprises from cereal boxes, packaging foam from mailed boxes, bricks, any-

thing that looks as if it has creative possibilities.

Construction Tips

Some may be frightened at the prospect of making or constructing the various items for these devotions. But rest assured, you need not be an artist to have successful results. Most of all, your children will appreciate your efforts, time, and especially the fun benefits they will receive. So be creative, colorful, and most importantly for your sake, enjoy yourself!

For nearly every devotion, I make what I have termed a "table marker." On two 3" x 5" cards, I write out with felt-tip pens (using different colors for variety) the verses that pertain to our study. Sometimes I use the same verse on both cards; other times I put different verses on each card. Using a third card as the base, I bend and tape the cards to form what looks like a triangle. (See illustration below.) This then displays the verses for a centerpiece on the dinner table that night. We have found this to be a successful way to introduce our devotion's topic and begin asking pertinent questions.

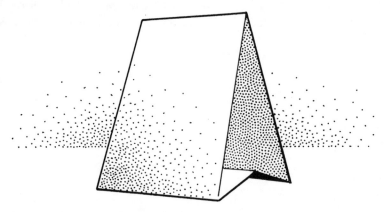

The Pattern from Joshua: Tell Them!

So often when I study the Old Testament, I find myself envying the richness of Israel's traditions and feasts. Passover especially is a wonderful example of a pattern for family devotions. It combined teaching history as the glorious story of deliverance from Egypt was told; true worship as the family thanked God for this miraculous deliverance; active participation as the entire family was involved in the preparation (their sight, hearing, touch, smell, and taste were all involved as they baked unleavened bread and roasted the lamb); and finally, it established firm traditions that the children must have eagerly looked forward to every year. Educators have spent decades attempting to duplicate this creative teaching pattern that God instituted so many, many years ago.

Joshua 4:1-9 provides us with another wonderful illustration to follow. Here the Israelites have just crossed the Jordan River and entered the Promised Land. They must have felt so hopeful, excited, and yet frightened concerning what awaited them in this new land. But God seems to set their priorities immediately: telling Joshua to supervise the building of an altar of twelve stones (symbolizing each of the twelve tribes), He stresses the importance of worship at that time *and* in the future. For the Lord tells them, "In the future, when your children ask you, 'What do these stones mean?' Tell them . . . these stones are to be a memorial to the people of Israel forever" (vv. 6-7).

Just what future is God talking about? The *children,* and their children's children, and so on. God has established a beautiful tradition and memorial that will be a perfect instructional tool for the families who will walk by this altar for generations to come. Can't you just picture it? Many years later a family approaches the area. The first youngster to reach the altar (probably the hyperactive one who never goes anywhere at a pace slower than a trot or skip!) stops before it in awe and wonderment. Excitedly he runs back to his father, grabbing him by the hand and urging him to hurry to this fascinating place. And he would probably ask just what God said he would: "Father, why are these stones here? What do they *mean?*"

As the children listened to their father retell the glorious story, certainly they didn't sit woodenly, bored with a dry tale. Instead, all of their senses must have been receptive and alive to this history of their people. They probably gazed intently at the river, possibly even sticking in their toes; the sight of the twelve stones would have triggered their imaginations as they pictured the leaders of the tribes gathering them; and the feel of the sun and wind on them may have had them wondering, "Was it a day just like this when they built the altar?" The stirring words, awesome sight of the stones, and active participation all must have combined to make this a time of family worship that the children would never forget.

Several years ago our family struggled as we crossed a river of great change. Realizing that we all had lessons to learn about faith in tough times, I asked God for wisdom and then dusted off our wedding candle. It would become our focal point for family worship—our altar. Everyone picked a small stone, and as we held them in our hands, we talked about how our faith was actually more real than these mere rocks. Pressing them between our fingers, we all learned a lesson about temporal things versus eternal reality. Then, placing those rocks around that lighted candle, we built an altar that represented God's presence in our family. Through those weeks of tension and worry, that candle with its odd-shaped, ordinary rocks became a constant source of encouragement for all of us. Later we would again gather around that candle to praise God for answering our prayers. Little did I know, though, what a continuing symbol that little altar would be for our family. Sitting in a prominent place in our living room, our candle is a constant memorial of God's past, present, and future faithfulness. No serious family worship in the Williford home would be complete without that special altar.

When my world gets out of perspective—when the everydayness and busyness of our lives threaten to sweep away my commitment to our family worship—I just go look at that candle. Often I pick up one of those rocks, rubbing it between my fingers once again. The memories that wash over me fill me with joy and a clearly focused perspective. A perspective that says *nothing* in this world is more important than creating an environment for worship of my Lord within this home. *Nothing* is more worthwhile than striving to help my sons grow spiritually. *Nothing* is more beneficial for our sons than time spent with Dad and Mom—and God. That ordinary candle calls us to worship Him as a family. Have you provided an altar that prompts your children to ask, "What does living a Christian life *mean,* Mom and Dad?" Build one.

Notes

1. *Lawrence O. Richards,* Creative Bible Teaching *(Chicago: Moody Press, 1980), pp. 108–11.*

2. *David C. Rudd, " 'Child-like' Attitude May Give New Meaning to Seder,"* Chicago Tribune, *6 April 1990, sec. 2, p. 7, col. 1.*

3. *Rudd, p. 7, col. 2.*

4. *Rudd, p. 7, col. 2.*

Two
BIBLE STORIES AND CONCEPTS

PROVERBS: CARRYING EXCESS BAGGAGE

MATERIALS NEEDED:
- [ ] bricks (one for each member of the family)
- [ ] sturdy sacks (for carrying the bricks, one per person)
- [ ] broad felt-tip marker or crayon (black or red)
- [ ] 3" x 5" file cards
- [ ] tape
- [ ] pens or pencils
- [ ] favorite family dessert
- [ ] Bibles

TEXT: Proverbs 12:25; 18:5-9; 1 Peter 5:5-9

PREPARATION:
- [ ] On each brick write in bold letters the word *WORRY.*
- [ ] Place each brick in a separate sack. (You may need to first wrap the brick in newspaper so that the sack's contents are still disguised.)
- [ ] Give each member of the family his or her sack *on the morning of the day that you will do this family devotion.* (NOTE: You will probably *not* want to do this on a school day— or any other day that would cause embarrassment to a child—as the sacks are to be carried wherever the bearer goes until that evening when you have your family time. Our family did this during spring break.)
- [ ] Construct a table marker, writing out Proverbs 18:5-9.

31

□ Study Proverbs 12:25 and 1 Peter 5:5-9.
□ Make special dessert, if necessary.

ON THE MORNING OF THIS DAY:
Give a sack to each member of the family. Inform them that each is to carry the sack *wherever he or she goes all day long!* Tell them that they are *not* to open them until family devotions that evening!

FAMILY TIME:
1. During dinner, discuss the proverbs written on the table marker. (You may first need to explain that a proverb is a wise saying given for instruction.) Questions you might ask are:
- **Why is it necessary to control what we say?** (our words can cause arguments, angry physical responses, trouble to our very souls, and display our foolishness)
- **Have you ever said something that you instantly regretted, wishing you could take it back? What did you do?**
- **When was the last time someone said something that made *you* angry? What did you do then? What does the proverb say about the hurt that gossip causes? How deeply do our words affect other people?** Build interest by telling them that you will be *demonstrating* one of these verses!

2. Surprise your family with a favorite dessert. Be sure to emphasize that our demonstration is this: just like we eat a dessert, gossip can unfortunately be devoured and digested in the same way. It does indeed go deep to the inside or heart of the hearer *and* speaker.

3. Later, begin your family time with prayer.

4. Explain that now we will be discussing a different proverb. Ask questions such as,
- **Are you tired of carrying around these sacks? Was it a nuisance? Did it slow you down? Are you ready to get rid of it? What if you had to carry it *all the time?***

5. Have everyone open the sacks. Ask, **What does the brick say? How do you feel knowing you've carried around *worry* all day?** (frustrated maybe? embarrassed? surprised?)

6. Ask everyone to look up Proverbs 12:25; have someone read

it aloud. Discuss the idea that if we're worried or anxious about something, this is just like carrying excess baggage—just like hauling around this brick! You may want to ask, **Don't worries feel heavy like the bricks? Don't they also slow us down and make us feel weary?**

7. Have everyone now turn to 1 Peter 5:5-9; ask someone to read this aloud. (You may want to use the alternative translation of "I will cast all my anxiety on Him, for I am His personal concern.") Emphasize that each one of us is indeed "His personal concern" and that we can actually *give* Him our worries. And, just as we were anxious to get rid of that brick, so we should be ready to give Him our worries!

8. Give everyone a 3" x 5" card and a pencil or pen. Ask your family members to write down *anything* and *everything* they may be worrying about. Emphasize that you are now attempting to *give* these worries to God; you are tired of hauling them around! Fold the cards in half to save; then, announce that you will read them again in six months for another family devotion.

9. Share one major worry out loud; pray for each other.

SUGGESTIONS:

Like so often happens, this devotion evolved from my need and conviction. Craig and I have often joked that, of the two of us, I'm the "designated worrier!" but though I can sometimes see the folly of my fretting, all too often I do let concern weigh me down. And that's when I go to 1 Peter 5 again—seeking His reminder to get it all back into perspective.

It was funny to see us lugging around those sacks all day. And yes, Dad dutifully hauled his off to church for work! I must confess, though, that I avoided going to the store that particular day.

By that evening all of us were quite anxious to be rid of those bricks—the very reaction I wanted our sons to know they should have in relation to their worries and concerns. Craig and I emphasized (for our benefit too) that we should anxiously seek Him in prayer, knowing without doubt that He is there, able and willing to carry what we cannot and should not. And just as we felt relief casting off those burdens, so can we feel peace and acceptance of circumstances by deciding to lay troubles at His feet.

When we pulled out our lists of worries six months later, we were indeed surprised how *once-heavy* burdens had now become mere memories. What a great lesson in perspective — looking at those worries from *this* side can hopefully make the things I'm fretting over now look just a might smaller!

GRIPES, GRATITUDES, AND GOALS

MATERIALS NEEDED:
- ☐ 3″ x 5″ file cards
- ☐ tape
- ☐ pens or pencils for each family member
- ☐ notebook paper
- ☐ Bibles

TEXT: Habakkuk 3:17-18

PREPARATION:

    ☐ Study the background of the Book of Habakkuk and chapter 3 specifically. (Suggestions for books to aid your study are given at the end of this book.)

    ☐ Construct a table marker, writing out Habakkuk 3:17-18.

FAMILY TIME:

1. During dinner, you may want to begin your discussion by asking,
- **Who was Habakkuk?** (a prophet of God)
- **What does it mean to be God's prophet?** (the prophecies— or pictures of the future—will *always* come true since they are from God)
- **In this Book of Habakkuk, what question does he ask God in many different ways?** (why do You allow bad things— unjust things—to keep happening? And why do bad things happen to good people?) **Do we ask these same questions today that Habakkuk wrestled with?** (Yes!)
- **Can you think of some examples from school when you've wondered, "Why does God let that happen?"**(the child at school who is always misbehaving and yet receives adulation from peers because of his or her athletic prowess)
- **What are some examples from the news?** (a pro-life candidate who lost the local election) Emphasize that though the examples are different from Habakkuk's, the questions are essentially the *same.*

2. Later, begin your family time with prayer.

3. Explain that much of the Book of Habakkuk is filled with his complaints. God appears to patiently listen, not explaining Himself (or what He does) but affirming His sovereignty, and amazingly, telling Habakkuk that things will actually get worse before they get better. However, God does allow Habakkuk this time of griping—a "clear-the-air" experience, it seems. Sometimes families also need a time like this to maintain good communication with each other and God.

4. Ask everyone to bring a chair away from the kitchen table; arrange them in a circle. Explain that there may have been times recently in our home when we wish another member of the family had said something differently. After exchanging chairs with that person, we will then have the opportunity to say, "I wish _____ (the person in whose chair I'm sitting) had said to me (or to another member of the family). . . . " Afterward, you should switch back to your original chairs. Everyone can do this exercise as much as the family needs and desires to "clear the air." (NOTE: This is *not* intended to be used as a battle zone! Instead, this presents a nonthreatening communication forum in which past hurts can be verbalized and hopefully healed.)

5. When everyone is done, point out that Habakkuk also praised God, showing us that along with our gripes must come *gratitudes*. Therefore, we will now verbalize this: "I wish that I had said to _____ . . . . " Remind everyone that these statements include compliments, congratulations, expressions of love and gratitude. (You will not need to exchange chairs this time, but you may want to look at the person to whom you're giving this gratitude.)

6. Ask everyone to move the chairs back around the kitchen table and be seated. Ask someone to read Habakkuk 3:17-18. Point out that now Habakkuk seems to have moved to *goals* as he firmly states, "Yet I will rejoice in the Lord, I will be joyful in God my Savior." And note that this is in the midst of all the problems he lists—fig trees with no buds, vines with no grapes, failed olive crops, fields with no food, pens with no sheep, and stalls with no cattle! Point out that Habakkuk apparently has learned the lesson of true faith: he has decided to trust God no matter what the

circumstances around him may be.

7. Give everyone a 3″ x 5″ card and a pen or pencil. Ask them to write at the top: My Personal Goal of Trust. Then, just as Habakkuk lists three major areas of complaints after the word *though,* have each family member list three "gripes." Conclude by writing out Habakkuk's goal of trust. For example, a child may write something like this: "Though I have a lot of homework to do, though our soccer team lost today, and though I lost my allowance, 'yet I will rejoice in the Lord, I will be joyful in God my Savior.' " Emphasize the choice we have to *decide* to trust God in the midst of our mess!"

8. Share your goals with each other. You may want to exchange them and then pray for that person's gripes and his or her ability to decide to trust God.

SUGGESTIONS

Craig and I seek ways to help our sons communicate openly and honestly with us, and that includes the levels of mere information, what has made them feel happy and hurt, and—though it may be harder to hear—whatever we may have done or said, (or *not* done or said) to make them feel distanced from us. We've found that if we don't make the effort to provide a forum especially for this purpose, this type of communication just doesn't happen; instead, feelings get stuffed deep inside, providing fertile soil for even minor resentments to grow into major walls of silence.

Using this type of format was nonthreatening for us, and we all gained valuable insights concerning each other's hurts and needs. Some of the "I wish you had saids" were ones I had expected; others were a surprise to me—and those were the ones that made this format especially helpful. This devotion had opened new doors: conversations followed later which might have never happened otherwise.

Lastly, I can remember when I used to think that faith was this elusive quality; to truly be faithful I had to manufacture faithful *feelings.* Obviously, I was often frustrated when circumstances were awful—and all I felt was miserable! Later I learned that faith is indeed a decision that I must constantly make; I *decide* to trust

God today, regardless of the circumstances (and resulting feelings) this day may bring. If our sons grasped only this concept from our family worship, then our journey through Habakkuk has indeed been one worth traveling.

LESSONS IN NUMBERS: GRAVES OF CRAVING!

MATERIALS NEEDED:

- [ ] large piece of cardboard (to make a game board)
- [ ] coins or other small objects (for game pieces)
- [ ] felt-tip pens (black plus assorted colors)
- [ ] white construction paper
- [ ] scissors
- [ ] lined paper
- [ ] 3" x 5" file cards
- [ ] Scotch Tape
- [ ] pencils
- [ ] Bibles

TEXT: Numbers 11

PREPARATION:

- [ ] Prepare game board by writing "Graves of Craving Dictionary Game!" at the top of the cardboard. Using felt-tip pens, draw fire in the bottom left corner, twelve steps spiraling upward with "Gimme!" written on each one, and finally, at the end of the last step, draw a gravestone in the upper-right-hand corner with "Here Lies. . . . Rest in Peace" written on it. (See illustration.) Color the fire, steps, and gravestone as desired.

- [ ] From the white construction paper, cut enough gravestone shapes (approximately 3 " x 5") for each member of the family. (I always do one extra in case someone needs another.) On these write "R.I.P." with a black felt-tip pen.

- [ ] Also from the white construction paper, cut at least fifty pieces, approximately 3" x 5" in size. (Or, you may have notepad paper available.) On twelve of these, write one word from the list below and its definition.

- HOMER—60 bushels
- SEDULOUS—diligent, seeking diligently
- RESIN—a substance (which is clear and transparent) of plant origin
- ENVENOM—to fill with malice, be angry
- KIBROTH—Hebrew for a grave

- RAPACIOUS—greedy, ravenous with desire
- TABERAH—Hebrew for burning, on fire
- CORIANDER—a type of seed
- LACHRYMOSE—lamentable, mournful
- AGOG—keenly anticipating, looking forward to
- FAIN—ready, willing
- HATTAAVAH—Hebrew for a strong craving or desire
  ☐ Review these rules to read later:

a. This is a dictionary game; the object is to make up definitions for the words which I will give to you. Your made-up definitions should be either as close to the real meaning as possible OR meanings that *appear* to be the definitions. By guessing the correct meaning and/or winning points as others select *your* definitions, you will advance to the end of the game board.

b. The game will progress this way: I will pronounce and spell out a word for you. You will write the word on a piece of paper and then make up a definition for that word. *Your object or goal is to write a definition which other members of the family will believe to be the true definition.* After collecting everyone's definition, I will read aloud all the definitions, *INCLUDING THE CORRECT ONE.* (My goal is to fool you, hoping that none of you will guess the correct definition.) Then I will ask, "Which definition is the correct one?" Everyone will vote for ONE definition, attempting to guess the correct one.

c. Game pieces (either coins or other small objects) will begin on the fire drawing. They will be moved ahead by squares for the following scoring:
  - you choose the correct definition: 2 squares
  - someone chooses your made-up definition: 1 square
  - none of you chooses the correct definition: *I* get to move ahead 2 squares

d. The first person to reach the "Here lies . . . " wins!
  ☐ Construct a table marker, writing out Numbers 11:4-6.
  ☐ Read Numbers 11, studying background and content.

FAMILY TIME:

1. During dinner, discuss the background of Numbers 11, reviewing that the Israelites had been slaves in Egypt, how God

miraculously enabled Moses to lead them out and that they were now traveling to the Promised Land. Be sure to explain at some point that *manna* was the food that God provided for them.

2. Open your family time with prayer.

3. Announce that you will be playing the "Graves of Craving Dictionary Game!" (You may need to explain exactly what a craving is. Children may understand it best by reminding them of a current television commercial which makes them desire food, toys, etc.!)

4. Give twelve sheets of the 3" x 5" paper and a pencil to each family member. (As the one who reads these definitions, you will not need this paper.)

5. Read the game rules. Be sure to ask for questions, making sure that everyone understands the rules. You may want to make the first word, *homer,* a sample word.

6. Proceed through the words of the game, further explaining any definitions that may be unclear to children. When someone wins, you may want to emphasize that *all* were winners because everyone hopefully learned some new words!

7. Ask family members to turn in their Bibles to Numbers 11; tell them that *all* the words from the game were somehow related to this chapter—whether Hebrew or the English translation. (At this point, you may want the other parent to review this chapter, if possible.) Review the highlights of Numbers 11:

● the people's complaining and resulting fire from God (**What did the game board's fire symbolize? Do you remember what** *Taberah* **means?** on fire);

● wailing against manna (**The Israelites mourn for their former lifestyle, reminiscing that food was of great variety and free. Was it free?** No! Their very *selves* were owned by the Egyptians!)

● Moses' pleading with God and His answer (**What does God say He will give His people?** meat **For how long?** until they're sick of it! **Can you think of a time when you got too much of a good thing?** upset stomach after eating candy, a wild or spinning ride at an amusement park);

● the quail and the plague (**You learned what Kibroth and Hattaavah mean; what do they mean together?** "graves of craving" **Why is this a fitting name for this place?** because their craving—and therefore turning against God—caused their own deaths).

8. Remind family members that we also can crave things which can "bury" us in a consuming desire. We can complain so much about what we don't have (and possibly *can't* have) that we completely forget to be thankful for what we *do* have.

9. Hand out the pieces of paper shaped like gravestones. Ask everyone to think of one craving that is threatening to bury him or her with desire. Tell them that tonight we will attempt to bury the *cravings* rather than the cravings burying *us*. Ask each to write this craving on the paper.

10. Share these cravings and pray for each other, asking God to help us focus on the blessings that we do have.

SUGGESTIONS:

I adapted this dictionary game from one that we often play as a family. The instructions recommend that players be at least ten years old, so you will want to keep this in mind when selecting this devotion for your children.

The year we did this family worship was a particularly rough one. An emergency surgery, Dad's residency for an Ed.D. and the resulting depletion of funds left us merely watching everyone else go on vacations; yes, we craved—everything we couldn't have! We took no time at all to scribble desires on those tombstones, spilling out our frustrations and hurts too. By noting what we *did* have and then praying for each other, we seemed to gain a better perspective: one through God's eyes.

LESSONS IN NUMBERS: FAMILY BANNER

MATERIALS NEEDED:

- [ ] large piece of white felt (I used felt from a Christmas tree skirt; around that time of year you can find this at almost any store carrying Christmas goods)
- [ ] squares of felt in assorted colors
- [ ] felt-tip pens, all colors
- [ ] alphabet stencils
- [ ] dowel rod
- [ ] scissors
- [ ] glue
- [ ] nature books containing pictures of animals (large and clear enough to trace)
- [ ] tracing paper (most typing paper will be adequate)
- [ ] *The NIV Study Bible*
- [ ] access to a copier which enlarges
- [ ] Bibles

TEXT: Numbers 2; 3:5-13; Exodus 28:15-21; Ezekiel 1:10; Revelation 4:7

PREPARATION:

- [ ] Study Numbers 2 — the encampment and marching order of the tribes of Israel. In your Bible, mark the tribal names and where they were to camp. Also, review who the Levites were and why they fulfilled a unique role (Numbers 3:5-13).

- [ ] Copy and enlarge the chart on page 192 of *The NIV Study Bible.* You may want to make a copy for each family member.

- [ ] Collect materials for making a family banner: white felt (you may desire to cut this into a flag shape beforehand), various colored felt squares, glue, scissors, dowel rod, nature books, tracing paper, pencils, felt-tip pens, and stencils.

FAMILY TIME:

1. Sitting around your kitchen table, open with prayer.
2. Read Numbers 2:1-2 and then highlights of the tribal names

and positions; end by reading all of verse 34. (If you are reading from *The NIV Study Bible,* you may also want to read the note on v. 2.)

3. Place the picture of the encampment and marching order so that you can point out God's directions for His people. Be sure to emphasize the tabernacle's placement when at rest and the ark's position (and who carried it) for marching.

4. You may wish to ask these questions:

- **Which tribe contains the line of Christ?** (Judah)
- **Can you name the sons—and one daughter—by the order of their births and by mothers?** (Leah—Reuben, Simeon, Levi, Judah; Bilhah—Dan, Naphtali; Zilpah—Gad, Asher; Leah—Issachar, Zebulun, *Dinah;* Rachel—Joseph, Benjamin)
- **Why isn't Joseph present in the encampment and marching order?** (he was ruler over Egypt and his sons took his place)
- **Who were Joseph's sons?** (Ephraim and Manasseh)
- **Why is the tribe of Levi not part of the encampment around the tabernacle? And why are the Levites set apart?** (read Numbers 3:5-13, noting that the Levites were set apart in place of the first male offspring which would have been struck down in Egypt and that therefore they were to do the work required to care for the tabernacle) You may also wish to point out the leading tribe of each group, discussing why they were the leaders.

5. Read verses 1 and 2 again, noting that each tribe had a banner and each triad (grouping of three tribes) had a standard. Point out that Jewish tradition says that Judah's standard had a lion on it; Reuben's, a man; Ephraim's, an ox; and Dan's, an eagle. Ask a family member to turn to and read each of these references: Exodus 28:15-21; Ezekiel 1:10; and Revelation 4:7. Use these vivid descriptions to feed your imaginations.

6. Announce that since the Israelites had family banners, *we* will now make one for our family! After placing all of the supplies on the table, tell everyone that you must first decide on what figure or animal you will place prominently on the banner. You may want to ask: **What qualities does our family exhibit?"** (courage, spirit, inquisitiveness, and loyalty are possibilities) **What**

animal then seems to best portray our qualities? (a bear? a fox? a lion? an eagle?) Leaf through your nature book to find pictures of animals that you may wish to consider.

7. Once you have decided on an animal or figure, assign the job of tracing and then cutting out this choice to a family member. Others may be given the assignments of using the alphabet stencils to put your family name on the banner, cutting out various backgrounds (we put large and small circles of different colors behind our eagle), and then using the tracing paper outline to mark around and cut out your animal from the felt which you have chosen. Remember to let your children's creativity run fairly free: they may want to add other figures, Bible verses, or symbols. Glue the parts together. Finally, wrap the wide end of the banner around the dowel rod and glue it into place. (One word of warning: you may want to prepare little ones that your flag won't be ready for waving until the glue has enough time to dry!)

8. Close in prayer, thanking God for His preservation of the Israelite people—and thus the line of Jesus Christ—and for *your* family and its specialness which the banner represents.

SUGGESTIONS:

This devotion adapts well for those of you with younger children; just be sure to keep the instruction part short and the construction of your banner simple enough for their abilities. At the same time, older children will enjoy this one too as they review more specific details of the tribes and construct a more complicated and creative banner.

Making a banner seems to have a subtle and hidden benefit: we felt a sense of family pride and unity in its making and displaying. It now rests on the window sill in our family room, forever reminding us that, just as this flag was designed and put together by us, we too are a unit made and designed by God.

BONKER BATTLE

MATERIALS NEEDED:

☐ empty tubes from wrapping paper—enough for each family member to have one (We always have several of these after Christmas!)
☐ 3″ x 5″ cards
☐ Scotch Tape
☐ notebook paper
☐ pencils (one for each family member)
☐ felt-tip pens, black and red
☐ Bibles

TEXT: Joshua 1:9; 6:1–8:29; 9:1-18; and 10:5-26

PREPARATION:

☐ Gather wrapping paper tubes, felt-tip pens, pencils, and 3″ x 5″ cards for later use.

☐ On a piece of notebook paper, write out the four military battles and one battle of deception that your family will be researching:

- JERICHO—Joshua 6
- AI (the first battle)—Joshua 7
- AI (the second battle)—Joshua 8:1-29
- GIBEONITES—Joshua 9:1-18
- KINGS OF JERUSALEM, HEBRON, JARMUTH, LACHISH, EGLON—Joshua 10:5-26

Then, write out this list of questions which must be answered:

- Did the Israelites obey God? How? If your answer is no, then why not?
- Did the Israelites win the battle? If not, why? If so, describe the battle.
- What happened afterward?

☐ Decide how you can best distribute these five battles among your family members. (Craig and I took the losing battles—the first battle at Ai and, since the Israelites were indeed fooled, the Gibeonites. Then we all looked up the battle with the kings.) You may need to combine younger and older siblings.

☐ Study these passages yourself for background and answers to the questions above.

☐ If desired, construct a table marker, writing out Joshua 1:9.

FAMILY TIME:

1. During dinner, you may want to discuss Joshua 1:9. Remind your children that this command was given to Joshua, one of God's most faithful and courageous leaders. However, point out that since God reminded Joshua to be strong and courageous (and this exact phrase is repeated from verses 6 and 7), he must not have *felt* this way! Instead, Joshua evidently made the *decision* to obey God—and thus exhibited strength and courage. What an example for us to follow!

2. Later, ask everyone to bring his or her Bible to the kitchen table. Then, hand out pencils and 3" x 5" cards as needed. (Those who are doing more than one battle will need more than one card.)

3. Say that you will be assigning five battles (explaining that one is a battle of deception) to family members. Announce that, for each battle, we will be answering certain questions. Then read aloud the questions from your sheet, asking everyone to write these on the 3" x 5" cards.

4. Assign the battles, asking everyone to write the Scripture passages on the cards also. Allow enough time for family members to complete the reading and questions.

5. When everyone is finished, ask for the reports from each battle, beginning with Jericho. You may want to ask this question: **It seems as though God is trying to teach His people something over and over again. What is that?** (They must obey Him because He intends to preserve the nation Israel and *He is all-powerful*; God is ultimately the only One who wins any battle they will fight!)

6. Announce that now you will be handing out weapons for yet another battle—a "Bonker Battle!" Just before you hand a tube to someone, mark either a red happy face for a *winning* battle (Jericho, the second Ai and the kings) or a black *X* for a *losing* battle (the first Ai and the Gibeonites) on the tubes. The rules are these:

no bopping where someone could be hurt (in the face) and we will bop" each other until the tubes fall apart!

7. Move to a safe area to begin—possibly outside or in a large open area in a family room.

8. When the "battle" is over, assemble once again for closing prayer. Thank God for preserving His people, Joshua's example of obedience, trust, and courage, and finally, family fun!

SUGGESTIONS:

When I was growing up, one of our traditions during the Christmas season was a family battle with the empty wrapping paper tubes! So, I guess it was just natural for me to always save them in my family too. First Craig and I enjoyed bopping each other and then when the boys came along, they definitely added to the giggling, hilarious fun. If you have never enjoyed one of these harmless battles, you're in for a fun surprise!

Often we study Israel's success at Jericho while ignoring other lesser-known battles. The Book of Joshua pictures God's people in progress as they move into the Promised Land—obeying, disobeying, making progress, slipping backward. But through it all we see God's sovereignty and this was the lesson I desired that our sons learn. God is indeed in control over everything, and this reminder certainly gives us—and our children—peace and security in a time of continuing wars throughout the world.

DEDICATING A FAMILY MEMBER: PUTTING ON GOD'S ARMOR

MATERIALS NEEDED:

☐ resources such as *The Victor Handbook of Bible Knowledge* by V. Gilbert Beers (Victor Books: Wheaton, Ill., 1981) and *The Bible Knowledge Commentary,* New Testament Edition, edited by John F. Walvoord and Roy B. Zuck (Victor Books: Wheaton, Ill., 1983)

☐ cardboard (possibly from boxes)
☐ aluminum foil
☐ ski hat
☐ a pair of shoes belonging to the one being dedicated
☐ a belt belonging to the one being dedicated
☐ string
☐ felt-tip pens
☐ Scotch and masking tape
☐ scissors
☐ a camera, if desired
☐ 3" x 5" cards

TEXT: Ephesians 6:10-18

PREPARATION:

☐ On the morning of the day that you will do this devotion, decide which member of the family will be dedicated. (You might consider a dad beginning a new job, a mom who has just agreed to lead a program at church, a child who has begun a new school year, etc.) Then, after studying the information and pictures in books such as *The Victor Handbook of Bible Knowledge* and *The Bible Knowledge Commentary,* divide these assignments among family members:

● Verse 14—Using a *belt* belonging to the one who is to be dedicated, decorate it according to biblical times. Also, on a 3" x 5" card, write down specific ways this person will need to use this belt of truth in this new endeavor. Is this part of the armor offensive or defensive? (EXAMPLE: We dedicated Craig, since he was entering his residency phase of his doctorate. The belt was decorated with string to hold other parts of his armor. It is defensive in nature, and thus we charged him to remember—despite the busyness—his faithfulness and integrity before his family, his classmates, our church, and most importantly, his God—who must remain first priority in his time management.)

• Verse 14—Construct a *breastplate* of righteousness out of cardboard, felt-tip pens, string, etc. (Be creative!) Then, on a file card, write down ways this person will need this breastplate. Is this for offensive or defensive purposes? (EXAMPLE: Again a defensive part of the armor, the breastplate was to protect the believer's heart. Robb said this would protect his dad from the discouragement and frustration that having so much to do would bring.)

• Verse 15—Decorate a pair of his or her *shoes* like a Roman soldier's. Again, use whatever creative materials you may have on hand. On another file card, write down ways the footwear will help this family member to be "fitted with the readiness that comes from the gospel of peace." Will these shoes be basically offensive or defensive? (EXAMPLE: These shoes are defensive—to give the believer stability. We wanted Craig to find stability in Him and therefore know His peace—no matter how hectic circumstances might be.)

• Verse 16—Construct a *shield,* remembering that in Bible times they were made of wood overlaid with leather. On a file card, write down ways the family member will need to use this shield of faith. Is it an offensive or defensive weapon? (EXAMPLE: The shield is a wonderful defensive weapon, for its faithfulness would stop all the "arrows" aimed the soldier's way. Jay charged his dad to remain faithful to God and his family, no matter what weapons would be directed toward him.)

• Verse 17—Decorate a ski hat to resemble a Roman soldier's *helmet.* On a file card, write down ways he or she will use this helmet of salvation. Will it be offensive or defensive? (EXAMPLE: The defensive helmet was put on only when the soldier faced danger; therefore it gave him a sense of safety. We wanted Craig to always know God's presence and thus feel safe even amidst difficult times ahead.)

• Verse 17—Make a *sword.* On a card, write down ways this

sword of the Spirit—the Word of God—needs to be used. Is this part of the armor offensive or defensive? (EXAMPLE: Robb challenged his dad to use this sole offensive weapon in just that way. Continuing commitment to knowing God through reading His Word is a decision Craig would need to make to be ready for whatever might come.)

Again, be sure to read and study these resources mentioned, as they are invaluable sources of information for application.

☐ Study verses 10-13 also, so that you can begin with a firm "charge" to the family member being dedicated.

☐ When all the construction of armor is finished, hide these so that this may be a surprise later. Keep file cards with notes in readiness for later also.

☐ Construct a table marker, if desired. You may wish to write out something like this: "*(the dedicated person's name)*, prepare for battle!" and on the other side, "*(the dedicated person's name)*, we love and support you!"

FAMILY TIME:

1. Open with prayer.
2. Talk briefly about the special challenge ahead of the one to be dedicated tonight. Announce that the rest of the family desires to help this person in a special way, supporting and challenging him or her with an applicable portion of Scripture. Begin by reading Ephesians 6:10-18.
3. Explain verses 10-13, challenging this family member to make the decisions necessary to *be strong* (through God's power, which is unbeatable!), *put on* (with all urgency, and it is your responsibility to do so), and *stand* (not attacking, but defending against Satan's schemes).
4. Ask the family member to stand, announcing that now we will begin putting on" armor for him or her, preparing this person for the battle" ahead. (Whoever made the belt would now fit it around the person's waist, challenging him or her with the meaning and intent of the belt of truth. The belt-maker would then give a personal application for the one being dedicated.)
5. Proceed to put on the breastplate, shoes, shield, helmet, and sword. Give a challenge after each addition.

6. Take a picture of the soldier ready for battle!

7. Close with prayer, asking God to help this family member stay constantly ready with weapons at hand. Also, ask God to convict the rest of the family to always affirm and support this one just dedicated.

SUGGESTIONS:

Craig's residency (going to school full time for three semesters while continuing to work full time at church) loomed over us like some huge monster that was about to devour us; I knew we desperately needed to prepare ourselves for this in a special way! This devotion was the result, and it was a help. We felt supportive and yet also responsible for this upcoming endeavor: we had actively committed to be part of Dad's army" by challenging him in this way. Robb and Jay's applications were thoughtful and insightful; we all had taken time to think through just what these important concepts implied and specifically what they meant to *us* as a family. And yet we had fun with this too—Dad looked hilarious by the time we had him covered from literally head to toe!

You will want to keep this devotion in mind for all sorts of dedications, possibly eventually using it for each child. Certainly there are a myriad of activities that our children enter—with fear and insecurity, I might add—each year. What better way could there be to assure them that we'll support and encourage them throughout this time?

DEVELOPING SERVICE: COLLEGE STUDENT
CARE PACKAGES

MATERIALS NEEDED:
- ☐ recipe and ingredients for favorite cookies
- ☐ snacks of all varieties: hot chocolate mix, candy bars, chips, soup mixes, etc.
- ☐ addresses of two or three college students from your church
- ☐ stationery
- ☐ packing materials, boxes
- ☐ packaging tape and address labels
- ☐ pens
- ☐ 3" x 5" cards
- ☐ Scotch Tape

TEXT: 1 John 3:16-20

PREPARATION:

☐ Collect and organize all materials (pans, measuring devices, and ingredients) for making cookies.

☐ Set aside other "care package" goodies, boxes, packing materials, and addresses for later.

☐ Ask the students' parents for specific prayer requests concerning their sons and daughters. (We asked the parents to keep our "care packages" a secret too!)

☐ Have stationery and pens available for later.

☐ Study 1 John 3:16-20 and the definitions of love given in this passage.

☐ Construct a table marker, writing out 1 John 3:16-20. You may also wish to write out another table marker with "Love in Action!" on one side and "College Care Packages!" on the other.

FAMILY TIME:

1. During dinner, discuss the passage in 1 John after one of your children reads the verses. You may want to ask some of these questions:

- **God, through John, gives us several definitions for loving one another in this passage. Can you describe some of them?** (Jesus laying down His life for us; we Christians likewise laying down our lives for others; sharing material possessions with those in need)
- **What way does the Word describe as an "easy" way to love?** (with words or tongue—elaborate on this, emphasizing that we can too easily say, "I love you")
- **How then should we love one another?** (with actions and in truth)
- **Does that mean we should not tell one another of our love?** (No! But we do need to back up those words with actions)
- **Can you give an example of merely spoken words without loving action?** (infatuation—when a man merely looks at a woman and says, "I'm in love"; someone who says he or she cares for you and then offers you alcohol or drugs)

2. After supper, announce that you want to put love into action" by caring for some of your church's college students who are away at school. Mention that as a family we don't want to merely use words to say, "We love and miss you"; we want to act out our love by sending these special gifts! Share their names and specific prayer requests, elaborating on them until your children can identify with their needs. (You may be able to share similar concerns and needs experienced while *you* were a college student.)

3. Tell your children about the care packages" that you will be putting together, including homemade cookies, treats, and a letter from your family. Allow children to separate candy bars, drink mixes, etc., into the boxes.

4. Begin making cookies, allowing children to help as much as possible.

5. Meanwhile, place two to three pieces of stationery on the table (depending on how many students you are ministering to). Have each family member take turns jotting notes to the students.

6. When the cookies are done—saving just a few to enjoy now yourselves!—pack the boxes with cookies, treats, and letters, sealing and addressing them.

7. After asking for volunteers to pray for each of the college students, end your family worship by joining hands in a circle for prayer.

SUGGESTIONS:

We have done this at the beginning of the school year twice now, and I can't tell you the feelings of nurturing, caring, and love this activity brings! As we pack up those boxes (hoping that chocolate chip cookies won't get smashed beyond recognition!), we discuss how surprised and excited the students will be to receive our treats. Craig and I always relate how we dearly loved to receive mail—*any* mail—while we were away at college. A box of homemade cookies was *especially* cherished—and envied by every other student in one's room, floor, or dorm! (We've also advised our sons that the wise student does *not* open any box like this in the post office; he may return to his room with an empty box!)

We have also been encouraged to see our sons take to heart these students' prayer requests; they prayed for them with genuine concern and care. And finally, I think we acted out just what 1 John 3 tells us to do. It would have been easy to merely say to our college students, "We miss you; we love you." But by putting words into action—making cookies and sending them off to *show* we care—receivers *and* givers were blessed. College Care Packages have become a yearly tradition at our home. With the back-to-school purchases of notebook paper and new jeans, I find myself searching for sales on chocolate chips!

THE ANIMAL GAME!

MATERIALS NEEDED:

- ☐ balloons, 5″ in diameter or smaller
- ☐ large piece of poster board or cardboard
- ☐ felt-tip pens
- ☐ stapler
- ☐ darts (from a dart board), or for use with young children, pins
- ☐ dice
- ☐ yardstick
- ☐ pencil
- ☐ paper
- ☐ special dessert, if desired
- ☐ 3″ x 5″ cards
- ☐ Scotch Tape

TEXT: Job 12:7; occasions when specific animals are mentioned in the Bible (for example: Creation, entering the ark, the dove released by Noah, the frogs from one of the ten plagues, the loaves and fish used by Jesus to feed the 5,000, etc.)

PREPARATION:

☐ Make the game board. At the top, print "The Animal Game!" with colorful felt-tip pens. Next, if your children are older, you will need to mark lines to make boxes for *thirty* animals. (For younger children, cut down the number of animals so that they will still be challenged and yet able to give examples of these from their Bible knowledge.) The animals are:

- fish (repeat four times)
- lamb (repeat twice)
- horse
- calf (repeat twice)
- sheep (repeat twice)
- donkey (repeat twice)
- snake (repeat three times)
- bull

- bird (repeat twice)
- goat
- pig (repeat twice)
- wolf
- ram
- lion (repeat twice)
- camel
- dog
- frog
- ox

(HINT: If you're not quite sure where these can be found in the Bible, use your concordance to discover their roles! However, if you do need to look up some animals, try to do this *several days* before you actually play the game; if you're like me, your memory—or lack of it!—will put you on more equal terms with the rest of your family to make the game fair! Another option: you may want to use your concordance *during the game* when no one can come up with an answer.)

☐ Print the animals' names in small letters in each box. Then, after blowing up and tying thirty balloons, carefully staple the balloons over the animals' names so that they are concealed by the balloons.

☐ Make a tally sheet. On the top of the paper, write out these ways to score points for each team:

- PERSON GUESSES CORRECTLY—2 PTS.
- OTHER TEAM MEMBER HELPS—1 PT.
- PASS TO OTHER TEAM, WHICH ANSWERS CORRECTLY—1 PT.

Later you'll want to write team names on this sheet too.

☐ Decide on a *safe* area in which to mount the game board. (Remember that you will be throwing darts!) Mount the board temporarily to practice and judge safe distances to stand from the game board. You may want to mark this distance with tape. Then, remove the board to keep the game a secret. (NOTE: If you have younger children, you can merely take turns popping balloons with a pin.)

☐ Construct a table marker, writing out Job 12:7: "But ask the animals, and they will teach you!"

FAMILY TIME:

1. At dinner, ask children to guess what the table marker seems to indicate you will be doing for family devotions tonight!

2. Later, announce that you will be playing "The Animal Game!" and that animals can indeed help us to remember portions of the Bible. Divide into two teams and give the team members time to decide on names. (We chose animal names for our teams too.) Write these names on your tally sheet.

3. After posting the game board, read and explain these rules.

● Roll the dice to see which team goes first.

● One team member will then throw the dart, attempting to break a balloon and reveal an animal's name. (We gave each person three attempts to break a balloon.)

● This person must then NAME AN OCCASION WHEN THIS ANIMAL IS MENTIONED IN THE BIBLE. Each example may be used ONE TIME ONLY. (For example, the *ark* may be given only once.)

● A correct answer scores that team 2 points.

● If that person cannot recall an occasion, his or her team members may help. If the team gives a correct answer, the team scores 1 point.

● If the team cannot think of an answer, they must "pass" the animal to the *other* team. If this team recalls a correct answer (the entire team is allowed to confer), it scores 1 point. (If *no one* can remember an occasion for this particular animal, get out your Bible concordance!)

● Continue alternating team members' participation until all the balloons are broken. Tally the teams' points and award all players a special dessert!

● Close in prayer, thanking God for the important parts that animals have played in His plan.

SUGGESTIONS:

Our guys always enjoy a game, and this one was fun in that it combined active fun with a Bible review. They were good at it too—coming up with answers that I hadn't even thought of and remembering ones that I had reviewed and yet forgotten! Their guesses at what the evening was to bring (from the table marker clue) were a cause for laughter too; they were *determined* that we were going to somehow be taught by our dog Bojangles!

A few cautions: monitor the dart throwing carefully so that no one is in danger of being hurt and emphasize team *cooperation* over team *competition.* By providing a special dessert for all, we hopefully avoid that overly competitive attitude!

DEVELOPING COMPASSION: WALKING IN ANOTHER'S MOCCASINS

MATERIALS NEEDED:

- ☐ dictionaries (one for each family member, if possible)
- ☐ notebook paper
- ☐ pens or pencils
- ☐ timer
- ☐ 3″ x 5″ cards
- ☐ Bible
- ☐ Scotch Tape
- ☐ felt-tip pen

TEXT: 2 Corinthians 1:3-7

PREPARATION:

☐ Study the context and background of 2 Corinthians 1:3-7. Written to Christians, it addresses our suffering and troubles—which appear to be an expected part of the Christian's life—and need to receive and give comfort. God is the ultimate source of all comfort, and thus Paul encourages us to then allow His comfort to flow from our lives into those suffering around us. The word *comfort* in its Latin form means "to brave together."

☐ Set aside the dictionaries, a Bible, a timer, notebook paper, 3″ x 5″ file cards, and pens or pencils (one for each family member) for later.

☐ Construct a table marker, writing out 2 Corinthians 1:3-7. You may want to draw a picture of a pair of moccasins on one side.

FAMILY TIME:

1. Begin with prayer, asking God to help you be especially sensitive to each other's needs tonight.

2. Give a dictionary to each family member (or share as needed). Assign the words *compassion, comfort, distressed,* and *empathy* to be looked up. (You may wish to add the words *patient* and *endurance* if there are more in your family.) As each person reads his definition, discuss the word further and give practical

examples for each one. (For example, *empathy* means to so understand another's feelings that *I* feel this way too in compassion for this person. A relatable example might be a friend of your child's who was recently bullied on the playground. You might say something like this: **Can you remember a time when someone bullied you? How did you feel? Can you understand now how your friend felt? What could you do to help him or her if this happens again?**

3. Turn to 2 Corinthians 1:3-7 in your Bible. After reading the passage, you may want to ask these questions:

- **Who is the source of compassion and comfort?** (God) **What do these words mean again?** (repeat your definitions given earlier)

- **What appears to be one of the reasons that we have troubles and suffering?** (so that we may empathize with and then help others, comforting them)

- **The Latin form for the word** *comfort* **means to "brave together." How can we comfort someone by "braving together" with that person?** (by coming alongside that person—physically, making ourselves available for his or her needs; emotionally, attempting to truly understand his or her feelings; and spiritually, praying and supporting however necessary)

4. Point out that empathy—trying to know another's feelings—is an important part of compassion. There is an old Indian saying that expesses this very well and it goes something like this: To understand a man, you must walk two moons in his moccasins." (NOTE: I researched this quote very thoroughly, even asking the Library Service Reference System's assistance. Unfortunately, the quote's source remains a mystery.) Some say that the Northern Plains Indians used this expression. Notice too that the Indians had no understanding of a mile for that was not a word they used; instead, they judged distances by the sun's or moon's movement. You might want to ask, **What do you think this Indian expression means?** (you really have to attempt to *live* what another lives—or "walk in his shoes"—to understand another and have compassion on him) **Would you like to try to do this tonight?**

5. Hand out a pen or pencil and 3″ x 5″ file card to everyone, asking family members to write their names on them. Exchange names.

6. Next, give everyone a sheet of notebook paper. Explain that each of you will be attempting to imagine what it would be like to walk in that person's "moccasins." Ask everyone to concentrate very hard, thinking through all the responsibilities, troubles, and sufferings this person (whose name you have drawn) may have right now. Everyone is to write down, on the sheet of notebook paper, the feelings and accompanying troubles that he imagines that person to be experiencing. Also, ask family members to be thinking of ways in which they can comfort this person emotionally, physically, and spiritually.

7. Announce that there will be two additional "helps" to enhance your concentration on this person. First, we will all be moving to a place where that person (whose name we've drawn) often sits. (For example, a child may have a desk chair in his room or Dad may have a favorite recliner.) Second, so that we can truly experience "walking in another's shoes," ask family members to EXCHANGE SHOES with those whose names they've drawn. (I realize that Dad's ability to put on a child's shoe could be quite difficult, but he should do the best he can—sticking shoes on his big toes if necessary! Remember that this adds that needed bit of fun to the evening!)

8. Set the timer for 5–10 minutes (depending on the ages of your children and how wiggly they are), telling your family to listen for the timer. When the timer rings, everyone should return to the table. Send them off with a paper, pens, or pencils, and someone else's shoes on!

9. After the time has expired, ask everyone to share what he judges his person must be feeling and experiencing at this time. Then, ask them to share ways in which this person might be comforted. You might want to ask questions like these: **Could you really imagine what it might be like to walk in this person's shoes? Did it help to take time to put yourself in his or her place? Could this be a helpful way to know what others might be experiencing too—especially those whom we don't especially get along with? What about those who**

seem unhappy? Critical? Insecure? Selfish? Can you see how this could be a useful tool for really helping others?

10. While holding hands, take turns praying for each other and the special needs that you may have been able to identify while "walking in another's moccasins."

SUGGESTIONS:

Hopefully we try to understand our friends and loved ones in this manner all the time, but what about those who have a particular knack for "grating on our nerves"? And what of those who work out their unhappiness by being grumpy, critical, or just plain mean? I've found the best way for me to begin to feel compassion for these hurting people is to attempt to understand *why* — to try to see and feel what they may be experiencing. And this is what I've attempted to teach my sons too — when trying to understand the teacher who seems so critical and unfair, the bully on the playground who humiliates others, and the class clown who attracts attention by constantly acting up. If I can teach them to try to "walk in another's shoes" and thus feel compassion, then hopefully they'll learn to look at others through the eyes of love — *God's* love.

Three
AIMING FOR TROUBLE SPOTS

WINTER BLAHS: "PRESTO-CHANGEO"

MATERIALS NEEDED:

- [ ] wire (I used the type for making corsages, found at craft stores)
- [ ] balloons, 5″ in diameter
- [ ] kitchen utensils (meat tenderizer, spatula, wooden spoon, pancake turner, etc.)
- [ ] masking and Scotch Tape
- [ ] picnic blanket and basket, if desired
- [ ] picnic supper
- [ ] 3″ x 5″ cards
- [ ] felt-tip pens

TEXT: Isaiah 40:28-31

PREPARATION:

- [ ] This game—indoor croquet!—should be played during the winter months. Around our home, January or February is a perfect time for a "pick-me-up."
- [ ] Cut and form wire into the shape of wickets used in croquet. Be sure to make them large enough for your balloons to pass through easily. (How many you make depends on how large an area you have to play in. We played on the linoleum kitchen and wood dining room and living room floors. If your entire home is carpeted, you'll need to experiment to see if indoor croquet is possible!)

☐ Blow up a balloon for each family member, plus several extra. If possible, give each person a different color.

☐ Review the basic rules of croquet (all balloons must go through the hoops to reach the end; the first one finished can then seek to hit those not yet finished), but feel free to make up any new rules for this unique situation!

☐ Gather kitchen tools for mallets. Have several available so that family members may have a choice.

☐ Plan your croquet course; however, unless you will be using a room which can be closed off, wait to put down your wickets. They are too easy to trip over! (This way your croquet is a surprise also.)

☐ If desired, plan an indoor picnic for dinner too. You may want to prepare foods such as fried chicken, fresh fruits, and brownies to pack into a picnic basket.

☐ Study the Isaiah passage; note that the word *renew* means "to exchange," as in changing into another set of clothes.

☐ Construct a table marker, writing out Isaiah 40:28-31.

FAMILY TIME:

1. Open with prayer, asking God to bless your time.

2. Ask children to read aloud the verses on the table marker. Lead a discussion, asking questions like these:

- **How does Isaiah describe God in these verses?** (everlasting, Creator of the very ends of the earth, beyond growing tired or weary, beyond our understanding)

- **What does our great God do for His people?** (gives strength to those who are weary, increases the power of the weak)

- **What does this mean then?** (that our God freely gives *us*, His creation, strength and power)

- **Do we know for sure that all of us will eventually grow tired?** (yes! even youths and young men will grow tired and weary) **Notice, however, that verse 31 begins with the word *but*. Even though we all will grow weary, what does Isaiah say we can do?** (hope in the Lord) **What hope is this?** (in His keeping His promises—to keep us until He comes again one day!) **Once we decide to trust in His promises, what will we receive?** (a renewing of our strength, soaring on wings like eagles, running without growing weary, and walking without being faint)

● **Let's look closely at the word** *renew.* **It means "to exchange"—just like changing to another set of clothes. Can you picture yourself changing your clothes, taking off the** *tired, old* **ones and putting on** *soaring, clean, new* **ones?** You may wish to pray as a family at this time, holding hands and asking God to help you all actively and decisively trust in His promises.

3. Announce that, just as you have renewed your strength and "put on new clothes," so are we *changing the season!* Though winter may be raging *outside, inside* it is now summer. Therefore, we will be having a picnic (inside!) and playing a summer game. (You may want to keep the croquet a secret as long as possible.)

4. Spread your blanket on the floor and enjoy your picnic!

5. Later, set up the croquet wickets by using masking tape to attach them to the floor; hand out kitchen utensils for mallets and balloons. Enjoy your break from the winter blahs!

6. Close in prayer.

SUGGESTIONS:

With help, even little ones can enjoy this game. And of course everyone will appreciate the creativity of a winter "picnic" on the kitchen floor!

Whenever Jay is asked to name his favorite family devotion, he says this one! I think we were all so tired of the gloomy weather and seemingly endless January days that this was the perfect prescription for those winter blahs. We all laughed at ourselves, each other, and our crazy dog—who barked and carried on about all those balloons the entire time we played!

Most importantly, I think we learned about making *decisions* once again too—decisions made in spite of what we may *feel.* For though we did indeed feel weary, we committed again to trusting God for His promises to us. We were renewed by "changing clothes" from old and tired to new and soaring ones. And the warmth and laughter inside our home reflected a change that had also occurred inside our hearts.

PREPARATION FOR TRAVELING: "PRESENT PLEDGES"

MATERIALS NEEDED:
- ☐ small box
- ☐ wrapping paper and ribbon
- ☐ 3" x 5" cards
- ☐ pens or pencils
- ☐ Scotch Tape

TEXT: a verse or verses which your family has chosen to memorize

PREPARATION:

☐ Sometime before your family will be leaving, decide on a verse or verses which all agree to memorize. Those families with older children will be able to choose larger portions of Scripture, while those with little ones will need to pick easier ones. Whatever the ages of your children, be careful not to overwhelm them with too much; let your choosing truly be a *family* decision.

☐ Once you have picked your family verses, write these out on a table marker. Work on memorizing these by dividing them into sections among family members. Then, while eating dinner, keep repeating the Scripture passage over and over until everyone knows the entire portion. (You may need to work on this several nights.)

☐ For the family devotion before you leave on your trip, gather together a small box, wrapping paper, ribbon, Scotch Tape, 3" x 5" cards, and pens or pencils.

FAMILY TIME:

1. Begin with prayer.

2. Announce that you will be repeating your verses over and over while on your trip so as not to forget them. (There are several ways in which you can do this. You may wish to have everyone say the verses *together* every time you go through a town, see a red barn, etc. Or, you may have everyone say the verses *individually* each time you get back into your car. Since our sons enjoy sitting up front with Dad, whoever sat up front — including Dad and Mom! — had to say the verses each time he sat

there. Be creative and use whatever works best for your family!)

3. Discuss how sometimes being in the cramped quarters of traveling together can make us irritable with each other. Announce, therefore, that we are going to write "present pledges." These will be *gifts* that we will give to each other—written pledges of things we will promise to *do* or *not do*. (Give some examples so that children will understand. For example, Dad may promise not to keep the air conditioning on high so that Mom won't freeze! Or, big brother may promise not to tease his little sister.)

4. Give each family member a 3″ x 5″ card and a pen or pencil. Allow enough time for careful consideration of individual pledges and then ask everyone to write his or her pledge on the card. Be sure to have each one date and sign the card.

5. Place the cards (without reading them) in the box; have family members wrap and decorate the "present."

6. Explain that we truly are giving each other *presents*—of ourselves. By pledging to be more considerate of each other while on our trip, we are truly giving to help our family.

7. Close in prayer, asking God to help us remember and keep our pledges.

8. Later, when you are either on your way home or after you have returned, open the present and read aloud your pledges. Hopefully you'll find yourselves thanking each other for a much more pleasant trip than it would have been without the pledges!

SUGGESTIONS:

Each year on New Year's Eve our family chooses a portion of Scripture to memorize for that year. When vacation time comes along that summer, we've found that traveling time to be perfect for repeating those verses over and over again. And because we do repeat them so much, we've found that we really do *learn* them—not just memorize them for the moment. And then too those verses become entwined with the sweet memories of fun times spent together; just thinking of past years' family verses brings such warm and loving feelings!

My family responded well to the pledges too; putting signatures on those cards seemed to add a real sense of responsibility to this commitment. We waited until we were home to open the box—a small treat after the end of a fun trip! But most of the pledges written on those cards were not really a surprise; we had definitely noticed a change in our sons' behavior toward each other. Craig had pledged to not rush us out the door (which he accomplished the best that Craig is able to!) and I promised to try very hard not to nag or yell *and* to give up my favorite car-traveling activity—and the boys' *least* favorite—applying nail polish!

NEW SCHOOL YEAR: "THREE-STRAND CORD"

MATERIALS NEEDED:
- ☐ heavy thread
- ☐ masking tape
- ☐ Scotch Tape
- ☐ 3" x 5" cards
- ☐ pens or pencils and felt-tip pens

TEXT: Ecclesiastes 4:7-12

PREPARATION:

☐ Find thread that, though thicker than normal thread, can still be broken by stretching it tightly between your hands. Cut several 12" pieces (the number in your family times four, plus several extra). Practice braiding three of these by first taping the ends onto a table with masking tape. Then, test your "three-strand cord"; it should now be *unbreakable* (or extremely hard to break) when stretching it between your hands. Set aside thread and masking tape for later. (NOTE: A bright-colored thread is helpful for this activity.)

☐ Set aside a 3" x 5" card for each family member; you will use these to draw names for Secret Pals.

☐ Study the background and meaning of Ecclesiastes 4. Remember that the author—probably Solomon—speaks as a seasoned and mature teacher. Evaluating man, he tells us that life without God at its very core has no meaning. Pleasures should be viewed as merely *gifts* from God; they should not be our main pursuits, nor do they give meaning to our lives of themselves. With this context in mind, we learn that Solomon is teaching us about the meaninglessness of a life lived without relationships—with each other and with God.

☐ Construct a table marker, writing out Ecclesiastes 4:7-12 or verses 9-12.

FAMILY TIME:

1. After everyone brings a Bible to the table, begin with prayer, asking God to help you understand His Word.

2. Ask children to take turns reading through Ecclesiastes 4:7-12. Explain the background and context of this chapter. Then you may want to ask questions like,

- **Solomon continues to talk about meaningless or empty pursuits. What does he say is meaningless in verses 7 and 8?** (toiling for wealth, and especially so when all alone; be sure to remind your children how wealthy Solomon was)
- **The beginning of verse 9 says that two are better than one. Why?** (they can do more work together, they can help each other when one falls, they can help each other stay warm, they can defend each other and a three-strand cord is especially strong)
- **How can two do more work than one?** (cooperation! You may want to give a specific example—like two lifting a heavy object)
- **When Solomon talks about one falling down, does he mean only *literally* falling down?** (no, for anyone needing help looks to another to "help him up"; you may want to give a relatable example with which your children would be familiar)
  - **What about keeping warm? What can that mean?** (providing for another's *physical* needs—shelter, nourishment, clothing)
- **Does defending another refer to merely physical fighting?** (no, for hurtful words can be terribly overpowering unless we have a loyal friend whom we can count on to always be there to help)
- **The last part of verse 12 speaks of a cord of *three* strands while verse 9 talked about two friends. Who could this third person be?** (another friend—or *God*)

3. Announce that now you are going to *demonstrate* Solomon's conclusion concerning a cord of three strands. Give everyone a 12″ piece of thread. Ask them to break the thread. Then, give each family member three lengths of thread; help everyone attach these to the table with masking tape. Braid the three threads together. (Be sure to help little ones with this task, teaching and assisting as necessary. This can be a great educational tool for fine motor and eye-to-hand coordination.) Tie the end in a

knot when finished. After removing the masking tape, tie this end also. Ask family members to now attempt to break *this* three-strand cord!

4. Tell your children something like this: **As you enter this new school year, there may be times when you feel alone—when you may "fall down" in some way, when you will have needs, when someone may say hurtful words to you. I (or we parents) want you to know that *I am always here for you.* I will be here to "pick you up," to help with your needs and to encourage and support you. But *most importantly,* God will *always* be there with you—at times when I cannot. You, God, and I form a three-strand cord that is very strong and *cannot* be quickly broken. I love you. *God* loves you!**

5. Give a 3" x 5" card and pen or pencil to everyone. Have them write their names on the cards. Fold these in half and draw names. (You may wish to draw them from a sack, bowl, or hat.)

6. Announce that this person whose name you have drawn is now your Secret Pal. Do not tell what name you have! You are to be especially responsible for supporting and praying for this family member. Ideas for actively supporting this person are: surprise cards or notes of encouragement, small gifts—candy bars, gum, or mints, baseball cards, Christian books, etc. (Our family keeps this Secret Pal for about three months and then we draw names again.)

7. Ask family members for prayer requests pertaining to this new school year—adjusting to new teachers, feeling lonely or lost at a new school, making new friends, etc. Join hands and pray for each other.

SUGGESTIONS:

Every new school year presents uncertainties and fears that look like a deep chasm that threatens to swallow my sons. How I want to protect and shield them from all the hurts that are sure to come! And yet I know that is not within my responsibility as a parent: I should not become a bodyguard" who trails behind them, nor should I even attempt to protect them from all hurts—for these can be growth times used by God to build them into the men He intends them to be.

However, I do want to remind them at the beginning of every year (and constantly thereafter) that Craig and I are praying for them, supporting them, encouraging them in every way possible. And most importantly, I want them to know that God is *always* with them, always loving them.

Yes, we start every school year with new notebooks that are not yet dog-eared, new pencils that have full erasers, and new sneakers without holes. But we've found this to be equally important: new reminders of God's and our encouragement, support, and love.

NEW SCHOOL YEAR: "DEVELOPING WHISKERS"

MATERIALS NEEDED:

- [ ] the book *Taking Care of Your Dog: A Complete Guide to Your Dog's Medical Care* by Sheldon L. Gerstenfeld. (Reading, Mass.: Addison-Wesley Pub. Co., 1979.) If you cannot locate this book or if your family has a cat or other type of pet, you may wish to find another resource that explains the purpose of an animal's whiskers.
- [ ] dice
- [ ] notebook paper
- [ ] pens or pencils
- [ ] a mug (I asked everyone to choose a favorite one) and spoon for each family member (The spoons need to be of equal size.)
- [ ] bowl
- [ ] Bibles
- [ ] measuring cup
- [ ] 3" x 5" file cards
- [ ] Scotch Tape
- [ ] felt-tip pens

TEXT: Colossians 3:12-14 and Ephesians 4:2-3

PREPARATION:

- [ ] Construct a table marker, writing "Developing Whiskers!" on each side.
- [ ] Study the background and context of these passages in Colossians and Ephesians.
- [ ] Set aside notebook paper, pens, dice, mugs, spoons, and measuring cup (you'll need the ½-cup measurement) for later.
- [ ] Think about areas in which your children will have special needs or concerns this school year. You may want to think in terms of every subject (including lunchtime and recess) or for older children, every class or teacher.
- [ ] Note these game rules to be read later:

- Give everyone a mug and spoon; measure ½ cup water (*exactly!*) into each mug. Put an empty bowl in the middle of the table.
- Roll the dice to see who goes first; proceed clockwise, taking turns. Anyone may *pass* on a turn.
- On your turn, use your sensitivity or "whiskers" to give a specific area in which _____ or _____ (insert children's names) may have concerns or problems that you will try to be sensitive to this school year.
- After you give your concern, *carefully* spoon *one teaspoon* of water from your mug into the empty bowl. Note: You may not move the mug and bowl closer together!
- If you spill—even just a drop!—you must put one teaspoon of water (from the tap) back into your mug.
- Keep taking turns listing concerns or problems by using your "whiskers" until someone empties his or her mug. This person wins the "Best Whiskers" Award!

☐ Find the book *Taking Care of Your Dog* by Sheldon L. Gerstenfeld (or another book with similar information) at your local library. Dr. Gerstenfeld writes that a dog's whiskers are sensitive feelers. (This information is on page 17.)

FAMILY TIME:

1. During dinner you may want to capture interest in this evening's devotion by asking questions like, **What do you suppose tonight's family worship is about?! What kind of whiskers do you think we're going to discuss? And who do you think needs to develop whiskers in our family?**

2. Later, after asking everyone to get a Bible, begin your devotional time with prayer.

3. Ask part of the family to look up Ephesians 4:2-3; have the others look up Colossians 3:12-14. After these have been read aloud, you may want to ask questions like, **What words are repeated in both of these passages?** (humble/humility, gentle/gentleness, patient/patience, bear with each other, love, and unity) **What do you think it means to "bear with each other"?** (being sensitive to another's needs, problems, and concerns—and helping that person with them) **How can we develop**

this sensitivity or understanding of another person's problems? (we need to constantly be alert to areas which can be hurtful to those closest to us—and inquire about these things) **Can we do these things in our family? How, specifically?** (an example may be a shy child who feels intimidated by classmates at school; family members can respond by sensitively "bearing with" or helping to carry that burden by encouraging, listening to, and praying for him or her)

4. Announce that tonight we want to work on ways to really develop this sensitivity to each other. (At this point, if you have a pet you may want to point out your pet's whiskers!) Using the book *Taking Care of Your Dog,* discuss the information on a dog's whiskers—their sensitivity as "feelers" to navigate, especially in the dark. Tell your family that you all need to work on growing whiskers of sensitivity to each other—to know each other's needs and problems and how to help. (If necessary, give more specific examples to explain this concept.)

5. On notebook paper, write out either subject, class, or teacher lists for each child. As you go through the lists, ask each child to give specific concerns, needs, or problems (or *potential* problems) for each subject, class, and teacher. (Parents, you may need to give examples and add to your children's responses.)

6. Announce that now you'll be playing a game designed to further help everyone develop whiskers! Get out dice, mugs, spoons, measuring cup, and bowl; read the rules and ask for any clarifications or questions. Be sure to emphasize that, when it is my turn, I will attempt to say how *I personally* will develop sensitive whiskers for this person from the list that we made. For example, if a child listed social studies as his least favorite subject, an older sibling might say: "Social studies has always been easy for me. I will help my younger brother with his homework." He would then put a teaspoon of water in the bowl.

7. After the game has ended, exchange names and pray aloud for each other.

SUGGESTIONS:

Some concepts in this devotion call for older children; however, you can still adapt the basic ideas for younger ones. Even a seven-year-old can understand the need to pray for a sibling who is struggling with problems—relational and educational. And feel free to change the amount of water (more or less than ½ cup) or game rules (do away with the spilling penalty) for differing ages of children. If your children are young enough, you may even want to paint whiskers on all of you!

SELFISHNESS: "GIMME SYNDROME"

MATERIALS NEEDED:

- [ ] candy bars or other small candies
- [ ] dog biscuits
- [ ] buttons
- [ ] other small gifts your family members would enjoy (NOTE: For our family of four, I wrapped twelve gifts. You may want more or less depending on your family size.)
- [ ] wrapping paper, ribbon
- [ ] Scotch Tape
- [ ] a basket or box (large enough to hold the wrapped presents)
- [ ] dice
- [ ] 3" x 5" file cards
- [ ] Bible
- [ ] felt-tip pens

TEXT: Genesis 30:22-24

PREPARATION:

- [ ] Gather small gifts (candy bars, dog biscuits, buttons, etc.) and wrap them so that the contents are disguised. (You may want to make the dog biscuits and buttons appear to be the most enticing!) Arrange these presents in a basket or box; set it and the dice aside for later.

- [ ] Prepare a review of the history of Jacob and Esau for your children. You may want to consider asking questions like these: **Who was Jacob and Esau's father?** (Isaac) **What happened when it was time for Isaac to give Esau the oldest son's blessing?** (Rebekah helped Jacob trick his father) **How?** (Rebekah eavesdropped to hear Isaac's request for game, so she helped Jacob prepare tasty food and put goatskins on his arms to resemble Esau) **After Jacob received the blessing, what did he do then?** (because Esau was so angry, Jacob fled to his Uncle Laban's in Haran) **What exciting thing happened to Jacob on his way to Haran?** (he dreamed of the ladder to heaven) **What**

further adventures occurred once Jacob reached Laban's? (Jacob agreed to work for seven years so that he might marry Rachel, Laban's younger daughter) **Now whose turn was it to be tricked?** (Jacob's—for Laban gave him the elder Leah instead) **Can you name all of Jacob's children?** (Reuben, Simeon, Levi, Judah, Dan, Naphtali, Gad, Asher, Issachar, Zebulun, *daughter* Dinah, Joseph, and Benjamin)

☐ Construct a table marker, writing out Genesis 30:22-24.

FAMILY TIME:

1. During dinner, lead a discussion and review of the history of Jacob up to chapter 30 of Genesis. Ask as many detailed questions as your children's ages will allow. Be sure to let *them* tell the story as much as possible.

2. Later, begin your family worship time with prayer.

3. Announce that you will be playing a new game called the "Gimme Syndrome." (You may need to explain that a *syndrome* is something like a disease—a disease of *habits*.) Get out the basket of presents and dice. First, ask everyone to choose *one* present. After rolling the dice to see who goes first, explain that a roll of the dice gives these directions:

- 5 or 7—you may trade a present with another person
- 9 or 11—you may trade your present for one from the basket
- 4 or 8—you may take another present from the basket
- 3, 6, 10 or doubles—you may open one of your presents

Once a gift has been opened, it can no longer be traded or taken by another player. Continue playing until all presents have been opened. (NOTE: Though I knew what the presents contained, I played the game anyway. Just be careful not to obviously give away those with less desirable contents!)

4. Ask someone to read Genesis 30:22-24 from the table marker. You will need to review the background to these verses—that Rachel was desperate to have a child, especially after Leah, Bilhah, and Zilpah had borne so many. After reminding your family of Scripture's intent here—that God *is* faithful to Rachel in keeping His promise to her and thus also to the nation of Israel—You may want to ask questions like

- **What two comments by Rachel are recorded here?** ("God

has taken away my disgrace" and "May the Lord add to me another")

● **Do you know what the name *Joseph* means?** (it means "may He add") **What does this seem to say about Rachel? Does she seem able to truly rejoice in Joseph's birth — or is she already looking ahead to the future?** (she seems to have nearly forgotten that God has answered her prayers by *immediately* requesting *another* child) **What might that say to us concerning gifts from God?** (that we should rejoice in what we have — not constantly and immediately ask for *more* when we have just received a blessing)

5. Take some time to discuss your attitudes and expectations exhibited during the "Gimme Syndrome" game. You might ask questions like:

● **Were you ever happy with what you had? Or were you constantly working to gain even *more* and better presents?**

● **Do we have the "Gimme Syndrome" in relation to the blessings that God gives us?**

● **Can we be truly thankful for what we have and not be always seeking to gain more?** Try to make the point that we can miss the enjoyment of what we *have now* if we're always greedily desiring more.

6. Close in prayer, asking God to help us be content with and thankful for *current blessings.*

SUGGESTIONS:

While studying through the Book of Genesis for my personal devotions, I was struck by Rachel's comment at the birth of her first son. After waiting so long for Joseph, I expected her to respond with tremendous joy and thankfulness to God for this blessing. Instead it seems her entire focus shifted — from thankfulness for what she has just received to wanting more. Did she truly take time to rejoice in Joseph's birth? I had to ask myself, do *I* take the time to enjoy and thank God for what I have — or do I also immediately want more? Can I go through life never really enjoying the blessings that I have by constantly focusing on what I *don't* have? I think so.

Hopefully your "Gimme Syndrome" game played out these

attitudes as well as ours did! We all got caught up in the spirit of "gimme, gimme!" very easily. Isn't it amazing how wonderful *another's* present always appears? And how enticing even a dog biscuit can look when wrapped in pretty paper!

SELFISHNESS: "CENTER OF MY WORLD"

MATERIALS NEEDED:

- ☐ access to a gym or a large multipurpose room—preferably one with an AWANA circle (NOTE: You will probably need to ask permission to use the room.)
- ☐ masking tape
- ☐ cardboard
- ☐ gold wrapping paper
- ☐ Scotch Tape
- ☐ scissors
- ☐ large paper clips
- ☐ typing paper
- ☐ a pencil
- ☐ ice cream bars—ONE LESS than the number of family members (or another favorite family dessert which is easily transported)
- ☐ Bibles

TEXT: Matthew 20:25-28; John 12:23-26; Philippians 2:1-11

PREPARATION:

☐ Take masking tape and scissors to the gym. If it does have an AWANA circle, put masking tape circles (one for each family member to sit in) at varying distances from the center of the AWANA circle. The idea is this: you want family members to be tempted to try to reach the center of the circle, but *they must not be able to do so!* Because we have four in our family, I put four circles near the corners of the square inside the AWANA circle. Craig's was the farthest away with Robb's, my and Jay's circles spaced closer at various lengths. These individual circles should be about two feet in diameter. Then, use the masking tape to put each one's initials in his or her circle. (NOTE: The rules for this exercise are that everyone may attempt to reach the prize at the middle of the AWANA circle, BUT *no one's feet may ever leave the small circle which is his or her "kingdom."* Therefore, to judge where to put each of your family member's circles, you may need to stretch out on the floor yourself, testing for proper distances! If your gym does not have an AWANA circle, mark where you will put the ice cream bars and then measure your distances outward for everyone's circle.)

☐ If you have children between the ages of 8 and 11 (younger ages will not grasp these conceptual ideas and older ones will not appreciate childish crowns), make crowns from cardboard. First, make a pattern from typing paper (the shape of a flattened crown before the ends are taped together to fit onto the head) which can be traced onto the cardboard. After cutting out the crowns, cover them with gold wrapping paper. Fit the ends together (keeping in mind that a smaller child's crown will need to be tighter) and secure them with paper clips.

☐ Set aside masking tape, scissors (for any last-minute repairs), crowns, Bibles (one for each family member), and ice cream bars to take to the gym. Keep all of these things hidden—especially the ice cream—so that they will be a surprise later! (NOTE: You will need one *less* ice cream bar than the number of family members because *you will be going without.* You will be doing this as an example of servanthood for your family.)

☐ Think through ways your children need to become servants—especially in relation to other family members.

FAMILY TIME:

1. After you arrive at the gym, begin with prayer.

2. Take each family member to his or her circle, asking each one to sit there. Announce that all are either kings or queens—and the area within your circle is your kingdom!

3. Hand out crowns and just sit for a while, allowing everyone to enjoy being a proud king or queen! Be sure to add questions and statements like these: **Isn't it exciting being king or queen of a kingdom? Each one of you is at the very center of your own world. How does it feel to know that as a king or queen you are indeed at the very center of your little kingdom?**

4. Suddenly announce something like this: "Oh! I almost forgot an important part of this evening's devotions!" Then, after putting the ice cream bars at the center at the AWANA circle—and out of everyone's reach—announce this too: "I also forgot to tell

you all this. Because you are kings and queens of your kingdoms and at the center of your worlds, your feet *can never leave your circle.* You must remain at the very center of your worlds!" Then, return to your own circle and sit down.

5. Sit for some time and watch your family attempt to reach the ice cream bars! If your children are like mine, they will use all types of creative measures to reach those much-desired sweets— including taking off shirts and tying them together for a lasso! Keep repeating the ideas of, "But you are king or queen of your kingdom!" and, "But you are the center of your world!"

6. After some time has passed, silently get up and retrieve the ice cream bars; take one to each family member. Then, instead of returning to your "kingdom," put your crown in the small circle but sit *outside* of it. To your family's questions and puzzled looks, reply this way: "I have stepped out of my kingdom—out of the center of my world—to *serve you.* Because I have done this, I can never return to being queen of my kingdom, center of my world. However, I do this gladly—for I wish to serve you in this way."

7. While family members enjoy the ice cream, continue to discuss what has happened. You may want to ask questions like these: **Don't we all often act like kings or queens, putting ourselves first as if we are truly the center of the universe? What are some specific ways that we put ourselves first? What are some words that describe my acting as the "center of my world?"** (selfishness, self-centered, self-seeking)

8. Give everyone a Bible; assign family members to look up Matthew 20:25-28, John 12:23-26 and Philippians 2:1-11. After reading these aloud, ask questions like these:

- **What is the opposite of being at the center of your world?** (servanthood)
- **Who was the greatest servant?** (Jesus Christ) **Just how far did Jesus take being a servant?** (His obedience was to death—even to the cross) **What then does Jesus ask *us* to do?** (become servants too)

9. Ask everyone to come to the middle of the big circle; hold hands as you sit together there. Announce that each of us needs to become a servant—to "step out of our circles" by giving up being kings or queens at the center of our own little worlds. Ask

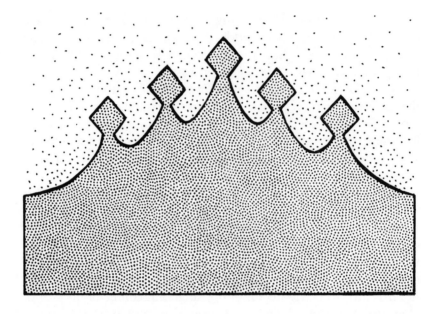

everyone to share on this question: **What is one way that I need
to step out of my circle and become a servant?** (You may need
to help younger ones with some ideas.)

10. Pray for each other and your desires to become the servants that Christ asks us to be.

SUGGESTIONS:

Each of us Willifords has a favorite family worship, and this one
is mine! The very graphic picture of the circles—and stepping *out*
of them—was an excellent educational tool for all of us. It was
amazing how wonderful it felt to be a queen at the center of my
own little world and then how much *more* joyful it felt to serve
my family in this way. *I* benefited from physically stepping out of
that kingdom; that visual lesson made an impact on me too!

No one needed prompting for ideas of ways to step out of our
self-centered worlds either. The guys caught on quickly with
heartfelt convictions. And our prayertime reached beyond the
usual surface needs of "Help Robb with his homework, help Jay
at basketball, and help Dad at work." Instead, we shared deep

needs for change that led to sincere intercession for each other. As I look back on this special memory, I am once again reminded why I constantly recommit to family worship. *This* is why I will continue this week and next week and so on!

NAGGING ELIMINATOR: "CONTRACT"

MATERIALS NEEDED:
- [ ] white construction paper
- [ ] pens or pencils
- [ ] sealing wax and stamp
- [ ] matches
- [ ] Bibles
- [ ] 3" x 5" file cards
- [ ] Scotch Tape
- [ ] felt-tip pen

TEXT: Proverbs 19:20

PREPARATION:

[ ] Think through areas in which you have found yourself nagging lately; these may be the very areas you need to address in your family contract tonight! Also, ask family members to think of areas which *they* feel frustrated about. For example, children may think some consequences are too harsh, bedtimes are too early, work distribution among siblings is unequal, etc.

[ ] Test sealing wax and stamp; set these aside to officially seal your family contract later.

[ ] Construct a table marker, writing out Proverbs 19:20.

FAMILY TIME:

1. Begin with prayer, asking God to help everyone be honest and open and yet loving and kind during this family discussion time.

2. Open your discussion time by explaining that you will *all* compose and agree on a family contract. This means two things: (1) this agreement will be discussed and approved by the entire family (though parents do have final say and "veto power" for extremes!) and (2) elements of the contract will consist of actions by all family members and consequences for these.

3. Next, ask for areas in which family members judge a definite or different consequence is needed for problem areas. You may want to consider asking leading questions such as these:

For children to consider—
- **What areas do my parents seem to be nagging about constantly?**
- **What punishments seem too harsh as consequences?**
- **What punishments seem unfair?**
- **What specific things are my parents doing—or not doing—which are very frustrating to me?**
- **What things are my siblings doing which are aggravating?**
- **What are some punishments, nicknames, or constant reminders ("Have you brushed your teeth?") which I judge I have outgrown?**

For parents to consider—
- **What things do I constantly nag about—which I'm *tired* of nagging about?!**
- **Which current disciplinary measures are too difficult or burdensome to enforce?**
- **What are some things my children do—or *don't* do—which are frustrating to me?**
- **What are some things that my spouse does which are aggravating to me?**

For all family members to consider—
- **What consequences are acceptable and appropriate for each child? Should these consequences be different for each child?** (NOTE: These are definitely areas for negotiation!)
- **What consequences are appropriate for parents?** (You will need to be creative here!)
- **Which disciplinary measures currently in effect need to remain in place? How can these be negotiated to be agreed on as appropriate if they are considered unfair by children?**

4. Specifically write out offenses and consequences on a piece of construction paper which has been entitled "(*Your family name*) Family Contract." Be sure to include differing consequences and offenses for each family member.

5. Ask someone to read Proverbs 19:20. Discuss how *all* of you—parents included—have benefited from this family discus-

sion. Point out, though, that gaining wisdom means *listening to* and *accepting* instruction. Therefore, mere participation in this discussion is not enough; actual *following through* on commitments listed on this family contract is necessary.

6. Add this statement (or something similar) to the bottom of your contract: "I agree to these terms and will abide by them to the best of my ability." Ask everyone to sign his or her name.

7. Use the sealing wax, stamp, and matches to add a bit of fun and make your contract appear official!

8. Close in prayer, asking God to help all of you keep your commitments.

SUGGESTIONS:

After hearing this excellent suggestion on the Minirth-Meier Clinic radio program, I knew this was just what we needed! There were several areas in which I found myself nagging constantly, and I definitely did *not* want to be remembered by my sons as "Mom the Nag."

However, though I had envisioned this as merely a way to agree on definite consequences for the guys' inability to do what I wanted, I was pleasantly surprised to see us experience a new forum for communication. The boys had legitimate opinions and gripes concerning a wide variety of frustrations—some of which I had not been aware of at all. I judge we were able to clear the air, discuss frustrations openly, and find general agreement on sticky issues because of this unique format.

Do be cautious in these areas: This is not a time for parents to "lay down the law." Children must understand that, though parents do have final say, their opinions will be heard and considered as valid. Also, don't let this progress into a mere gripe and complaint session. The purpose of sharing our frustrations is to find *solutions* to these problems. And do all sharing in a spirit of love—and sometimes, fun!

One of the offenses I wanted addressed was the "litter" left in the family room—dirty cups, sticky bowls, empty popcorn bags. The consequence for each family member differed greatly and showed the fun we had with this devotion. Robb's consequence is to do dinner dishes two nights in a row; Jay must sweep or dust the family room; Mom (yes, sometimes I'm guilty of this offense too) is to prepare a special dessert and Dad—this one is the best!—well, Dad is supposed to give Mom a back rub. Now that's what I call a fair and appropriate consequence.

MOTIVATIONS: "GETTING TO THE *HEART* OF THEM"

MATERIALS NEEDED:

- [ ] message and "secret decoder" pens from magic supplies at a craft or toy store (Or, you can use a clear wax crayon and several red crayons)
- [ ] notebook paper
- [ ] pens or pencils, felt-tip pens
- [ ] ruler
- [ ] stained, torn rags (one for each family member)
- [ ] Bibles
- [ ] 3" x 5" file cards
- [ ] Scotch Tape

TEXT: Isaiah 57:12; 64:6; 2 Corinthians 5:16-21; Luke 16:13-15

PREPARATION:

- [ ] Practice using the message and secret decoder pens (or clear wax crayon and red crayon) to make sure they will work. Draw a heart shape with the message pen or clear wax crayon; it should be invisible or nearly invisible. Then, use the secret decoder pen or red crayon to color over the heart, making it now visible.
- [ ] For each family member, use a ruler and felt-tip pen to draw a line from top to bottom on a sheet of notebook paper. At the top of each left side, write: "All the bad things that I do." At the very center of each of these sheets of paper, draw a small heart shape with the secret message pen or the clear wax crayon.
- [ ] Review the Scripture passages, taking note of how Christians should view good works and sin in their lives.
- [ ] Set aside decoder pens or red crayons, completed sheets of notebook paper, pens or pencils, and rags for later.
- [ ] Construct a table marker, writing out "Motivations— Getting to the HEART of Them."

FAMILY TIME:

1. During dinner, ask your children what the word *motivation* means. After some discussion, you may want to define it as "the

reasons why we do what we do." Point out that sometimes our motivations may be obvious and other times they may be very hard to discover.

2. Later, after asking everyone to get a Bible, begin your family time with prayer.

3. Hand out the sheets of notebook paper and pens or pencils. First, ask everyone to list "all the good things that I do." (You may need to help children get started by giving examples such as taking the dog for a walk, helping a sibling with homework, etc.)

4. Next, ask everyone to list "all the bad things that I do." (NOTE: You may want to wait about five minutes for each list, suggesting that family members write at least five examples on each side.)

5. Then, ask something like this: **What do you think all those good things are worth? A lot of money?** After some discussion, you may want to say, **I'm afraid they're not worth much. As a matter of fact, here's what the Bible says they're worth! GIVE EVERYONE ONE OF THE RAGS.**

6. Ask family members to look up Isaiah 57:12 and 64:6. After reading them aloud, ask questions like these: **What do these verses say about our righteous works or acts?** (they will not benefit us and are like filthy rags) Tell everyone to mark a big *X* over his or her list of good things.

7. Next, ask these questions: **What about our sins? Will God count them up and use them against us? In other words, will He keep track of each one, listing them to count like bad marks on a report card?** After some discussion, tell everyone to turn to 2 Corinthians 5:16-21. Ask someone to read this passage and then ask, **How do you answer these questions now? Does God count our sins against us?** (no, for God reconciled— brought us back to Himself—through the work of Jesus Christ) **What exactly does this passage say that Christ did with our sin?** (He who had no sin in Him became *our* sin) Tell everyone to mark a big *X* over the lists of bad things.

8. Ask everyone to now look up Luke 16:13-15. You may want to ask something like this: **First we learned that our good works are like filthy rags. Then we read that our sins have all been taken care of by Jesus Christ; we've been reconciled or**

brought back to God even though we are sinners. Therefore, we've crossed out the good things we do and the bad things we do. So what's left? What is Luke 16 saying to us? (God knows our motivations for whatever we do—for He knows what is in our hearts) **Can people be fooled about why we do things?** (yes, for they can't see what's in our hearts; people may praise what God knows to be wrong)

9. Give everyone a decoder pen or red crayon. Tell family members to color the center areas of their pieces of paper. Then ask,

- **What is the point then concerning whatever we do?** (what is in our hearts—our motivations)
- **Should we still attempt to do good things?** (yes, of course!—but we should examine our reasons *why;* we cannot gain salvation itself or more of God's love—we already have *all* of God's love!—through doing good works)
- **Why should we do good things then?** (because we love God and want to glorify Him)
- **Since our sins are not counted, should we then not be concerned about them?** (no!—we need to continually seek to become like Christ)
- **What should we do when we sin?** (we need to ask for God's forgiveness and then change our behavior)
- **So whether doing good or doing bad, we need to constantly study our hearts. How specifically do we do this?** (by reading God's Word, through prayer, and by asking for help and advice from godly people)

10. End by holding hands, asking God to help each one of you focus on his or her motivations and attempt to make them honoring to Him.

SUGGESTIONS:

When we received the secret message and decoder pens from a cereal box, I knew those pens contained a germ of an idea for family devotions; all I had to do was discover what that was! Thinking about the pen's revealing what was secretly there seemed to point to the idea of motivations—why we do good things and why we work to not do the bad. This struck me as especially important in light of the fact that for years I attempted to please God so that I could gain more of His love; I didn't realize He already loved me completely. Conversely, I also struggled with accepting His unconditional and continuing love when I sinned. This family worship brought all those ideas together and hopefully pictured them truthfully and correctly.

Remember that younger children will not be able to grasp these more conceptual ideas. So if those of you with small children have some of those secret decoder pens, tuck them away for now; in a few years you'll have a special purpose for them!

SELF-IMAGE: "INTERVIEW"

MATERIALS NEEDED:

- ☐ access to computer and printer or typewriter and copier (the interviews can also be written by hand if necessary)
- ☐ paper for interviews—one for each family member
- ☐ pens or pencils
- ☐ Bible
- ☐ 3" x 5" file cards
- ☐ Scotch Tape
- ☐ felt-tip pens

TEXT: Psalm 139:13-16

PREPARATION:

☐ Several days before your family worship night, make a copy of the interview for each family member. Our interview questionnaires looked like this:

INTERVIEWER: _____
PERSON INTERVIEWED: _____
Favorites:
- color—why?
- sport—why?
- season of the year—why?
- breed of dog—why?
- room in our house—why?
- game—why?
- famous person—why?
- place in the world—why?
- book (other than the Bible)—why?
- Bible passage—why?

Questions:
- What are you learning now about God?
  (Be sure to save enough room for answers between these questions on your interview sheets.)
- If you could do anything you wanted to, what would that be and why?

- If you could go anywhere in the world, where would that be and why?
- You have just been changed into another person of your choice for one day. Who is it and why?
- My favorite dreams for the future include myself doing what?

Be sure to tailor your interview to fit your family's unique interests and personalities.

☐ Construct a table marker, writing out Psalm 139:13-16.

FAMILY TIME:

1. Several days before your family worship night, give everyone a 3″ x 5″ file card and pencil, asking family members to write their names on them. Exchange names. Then, give everyone a copy of the questionnaire, asking them to interview family members sometime before the night for family devotions.

2. During dinner on your family worship night, read and discuss the portion from Psalms on the table marker. Be sure to emphasize how each of us was made by God to be unique and special. You may want to ask questions like these:

- **When did God design who and what I would be?** (before I was even born)
- **Does God make any mistakes when He makes a baby? Is anything He makes not wonderful?** (no!)
- **What does that say about His love for us?** (He loves each one of us very much—exactly the way we are—for this is how He made us to be)

3. Later, begin with prayer by thanking God for making each of us unique and special.

4. Ask everyone to get his or her completed questionnaire. Proceed to read the answers on the sheets. You may want to do this by one person sharing all of his or her answers before proceeding to the next person OR by having everyone share on a question before proceeding to the next question. You may also want to extend and enhance your time together by further questioning family members on certain topics. (For example, if someone gives an unusual answer or maybe appears to want to elaborate more, encourage him or her to do so.)

5. Take some time to point out the similarities and contrasts of family members' answers. Emphasize that each one brings his or her special interests, outlook, and abilities to the family—making you a unique and special family unit too!

6. Close in prayer by asking everyone to pray for his or her unique person that was interviewed.

SUGGESTIONS:

This devotion can accomplish so many worthwhile objectives. Not only did we get to know each other better and appreciate the uniqueness of each family member, but each of us also received a double blessing: we made another person feel special by being interviewed and we enjoyed being questioned ourselves. This devotion has the built-in potential to build up each other—certainly a need in any normal family!

HANDLING CRITICISM:
"SORTING THROUGH THE JUNK MAIL"

MATERIALS NEEDED:
- [ ] "junk mail" (unopened) saved from several weeks (I think I saved ours for two months as I wanted a huge pile to use!)
- [ ] stationery
- [ ] postage stamps
- [ ] trash bags
- [ ] Bibles
- [ ] 3" x 5" file cards
- [ ] Scotch Tape
- [ ] felt-tip pens

TEXT: John 15:18-21

PREPARATION:

- [ ] After saving a good amount of junk mail, sort through it, organizing it into like piles. (For example, put business letter-sized mail in one pile, large advertisements in another, etc.) Then make a pile of mail for each family member (yourself included) by evenly distributing the separated junk mail.

- [ ] Using stationery, write a note to every family member. Make each one a special letter that points out that individual's exemplary character qualities. Emphasize your love for him or her and that you will never stop loving that person. Lastly, point out that your love can never be completely unconditional because of sin's impact on us all. *God's love,* however, is totally unconditional and perfect; He loves us completely and always, just the way we are. Place each note in a separate envelope and address it.

- [ ] If you have written these notes several days before your family night, you may want to then stamp and send these letters through the mail. However, if other family members have access to incoming mail before you do, DO NOT RISK SENDING THESE LETTERS; the notes must be a surprise to their recipients for the devotion!

- [ ] Ask your spouse to write *you* a personal note (with the same guidelines as given above). Don't explain why; merely point out that this will be used for your family worship. (Note: If you are a single parent, you might want to ask one of your parents or a good friend to write a letter to you.)

☐ Continue preparing the "junk piles" by putting the personal letters almost on the *bottom* of the stack. You may then want to label each pile according to its recipient (so as not to mix up the personal letters) and then place each pile in a sack for later. (This keeps them organized and safe from being discovered before your devotional time.)

☐ Construct a table marker, writing out "Criticism!" and these questions on each side: "How does it make you feel? What do you do/say when it happens? Do *you* criticize?" Think of specific times when *you* have been criticized that you can share with your family. Attempt to give examples which were related to your being criticized for being a Christian. (For example: a boss who criticized you for being too honest with customers, thereby not selling as much as the boss desired. Or, you may be a stay-at-home mother who feels criticized by the media for not having an outside career.) Then, think through your replies to these questions and possible answers your children might give.

☐ Study John 15:18-21 and what it says about the source of a Christian's rejection by the world.

FAMILY TIME:

1. During dinner, read the questions on the table marker. (You may first need to define *criticism.*) Give your example(s) and then the resulting feelings, actions, and verbal responses. Realize that your truthfulness and open honesty in sharing will help your children to openly share also. You may want to ask these questions:

● **What is your immediate feeling when you are criticized?** (probably anger or hurt) **What are your feelings underneath this surface feeling?** (possibly rejection, loneliness, embarrassment, belittled, unimportant)

● **Why do we often retaliate when criticized?** (As a defensive measure—to deflect the criticism from *me* back to the other person)

- **What are some of the reasons that we criticize others?** (sometimes to actually help another, more often to hurt—and thereby make *me* feel better about myself and boost my self-image)

2. Later, after asking everyone to get a Bible, begin your family time with prayer.

3. Give family members their piles of junk mail and distribute trash bags within easy reach. (You'll be amazed how quickly those piles of mail transform and grow into *mounds* of trash! We found that we definitely needed those trash bags!) Enjoy the time you spend together as each of you opens the various pieces of junk mail.

4. When every family member has opened and read the personal letter (and finished going through the remainder of the pile), you may want to ask questions like these:

- **As we go through life, we receive all types of criticism, don't we? How is criticism like this junk mail we just went through?** (A good deal of it is not worth anything, we need to sort through what was said to us—look for "grains of truth" that will help us grow and change—and then *throw away* the rest!)

- **What did you find hidden in all that junk mail?** (a letter) **What does this remind us to do?** (remember always and especially in the midst of sometimes heartbreaking criticism *what God thinks of us*—that He loves us completely and always)

5. Ask everyone to turn to John 15:18-21. After someone reads the passage aloud, ask these questions concerning the source of some criticism:

- **Why do some people criticize us when they may not even know us personally?** (because they hate *Christ* who is recognizable in us)

- **Why are Christians so often "targets"?** (because we are different; we belong to Christ, not this world)

- **What should we do with this type of criticism?** (Remember *why* we're being treated in this way—because the one criticizing actually hates the Christ in us—and remember that *God* loves us) Discuss more as your family desires.

6. Close in prayer, holding hands as you pray for each other to withstand times of criticism.

SUGGESTIONS:

I knew that we daily received a fair amount of junk mail (with apologies to those in this type of advertising!), but the stack that quickly grew in two months' time was nothing short of amazing! I guess the way I always sort through the mail to find that hoped-for personal letter from a friend gave me the idea for this family devotion. It seemed to be the perfect visual picture of God's loving message to us in the midst of the world's negative one. And if my family enjoyed receiving those letters as much as I was blessed by *writing* them, then the devotion was a definite success.

EMOTIONS: "HOW DO I FEEL WHEN . . . ?"

MATERIALS NEEDED:
- ☐ several blank sheets of paper
- ☐ crayons or felt-tip pens (fine tip)
- ☐ one, two, or three pertinent questions

PREPARATION:

☐ Decide on some pertinent questions for your family members to help them describe their feelings with a picture. Some of the questions which we have addressed are:
- **What is my strongest feeling this week?**
- **How do I feel when someone in the family is grumpy?**
- **How do I feel about homework?**
- **How do I feel when I'm home alone?**
- **How do I feel when I'm pressured or stressed?**
- **How do I feel when I lose a game?**
- **How do I feel when (parents/kids) argue?**
- **How do I feel when Mom has to nag me to do something?**
- **What was my (happiest/lowest) feeling this week?**
- **How do I feel when (I, someone else in the family) won't talk?**
- **How do I feel when I'm already busy and someone asks me to do another task?**

Try to choose questions that are pertinent to the needs of your family by being sensitive to each individual's moods. When we noticed that our sons were responding negatively to our stressful week, we decided to find out what feelings they were experiencing. When playing a game became a miserable experience because one could not tolerate losing, we asked the question concerning losing the game. Sometimes we just want a lighter sharing, and then we'll write and draw a picture of the happiest feeling experienced this week. *Whatever* we share, the rewards of knowing each other's feelings better are always present.

FAMILY TIME:
1. Have everyone sit around the table.
2. Hand out several sheets of paper to each person.

3. Put many different colors of crayons or fine-tip markers in the center of the table.

4. Announce that family members will be writing a brief description and then drawing pictures about their feelings on a particular question. Explain that participants need to concentrate on digging out feelings which are "underneath their feelings." This means that rarely do we feel merely sad, mad, happy or scared. For *underneath* these basic feelings are deeper ones— possibly loneliness, frustration, lightheartedness, or insecurity. These *deeper* feelings are a true indication of what is really going on inside us.

5. Explain that the picture we draw should be a depiction of a situation that shows how we feel. For example, if I say I feel sad, and underneath my sadness I feel lonely, my picture might be a drawing of myself in a huge crowd of people—but I know no one and no one is paying attention to me. If I feel mad, and underneath this I feel pressured, I might draw myself in the middle of a vice that is closing tighter and tighter.

6. Ask the feeling question and allow everyone plenty of time to complete his or her picture.

7. When everyone is finished, share your pictures by describing the feelings and drawings. Repeat for other questions.

8. Close in prayer.

SUGGESTIONS:

I have repeated this sole devotion from my first book because it has been so extremely beneficial and useful for our family. We have unearthed concealed hurts and angers, resolved family conflict, and come to know each other's hidden selves through this valuable communication tool—experiencing insight, joy, revelation, and sympathetic understanding along the way. I cannot emphasize how much it has helped our family and therefore I again encourage you to attempt this exercise.

Craig and I learned this technique when we were a presenting pastoral couple for Baptist Expression of Marriage Encounter. This wonderful organization changed our lives by teaching us skills we had not possessed before: the ability to dig out feelings and share them with each other and our children. Too often we merely assume that feelings will be shared, even if we are conscious of their existence and try to be open. However, only when we actually *set aside a specific time* to share does this come about in our homes. Otherwise, these important feelings get lost in the hustle-bustle of every day. Remember too that feelings reveal the *person* behind them—what he or she is experiencing deep down inside. That is invaluable information to the parent of a hurting child, an angry child, or a lonely child.

Now that our sons are older, we often announce (possibly during dinner), "Tonight we'll have a 'How Do I Feel When . . . ?' Think up one or more questions which *you* would like to do with the family." In this way we give each member of the family an opportunity to address trouble areas, hurts, frustrations, or concerns. Because of these times together, I have gained incredible insight into my sons, my husband *and* myself.

Four
WORSHIP

PRAISE AND MANNA

MATERIALS NEEDED:

☐ small Styrofoam shapes (approximately the size of large marshmallows) that are used for packing

☐ a special bowl or other container to hold the Styrofoam

☐ family candle and matches

☐ individual candles for each family member, if desired

☐ 3" x 5" file cards

☐ Scotch Tape

☐ felt-tip pens

TEXT: Deuteronomy 8:10-18; Exodus 16

PREPARATION:

☐ Collect a bowlful of the Styrofoam packing shapes. You will want enough so each family member will be able to collect five to ten of these.

☐ Set aside the "manna," candle(s), and matches for later.

☐ Construct a table marker using colorful felt-tip pens, writing out "God's Manna to Us" on each side.

☐ Study the background of this portion of Deuteronomy 8: the chapter contains reminders to the nation of Israel to not forget the Lord. The command to not forget means actively *re-membering*—praising Him for the times in the past when God provided for needs in special and miraculous ways. Note the warnings to Israel against the pride of self-sufficiency; instead, they were to observe His commands, laws, and decrees while rehearsing that *His* power and strength provided for their needs. (NOTE: You may also want to review what manna is and when it was given to Israel; this is recorded in Ex. 16.)

FAMILY TIME:

1. During dinner, you may want to talk about *manna*—what it is, what it looked like, how it was to be gathered, and how the nation of Israel responded to God's gift.

2. Later, after asking everyone to get a Bible, begin your family worship with prayer. Light the large family candle.

3. Ask everyone to turn to Deuteronomy 8:10-18. You may want to ask one person to read the entire passage, have several take turns, or ask everyone to read in unison. Then, ask questions like these: **This passage is written to Israel, reminding the people to not forget their God. How do we actively *not* forget?** (by remembering) **And how specifically do we "remember God"?** (by verbally rehearsing His past blessings to us and praising Him for them) **Was this what the writer of this passage did for Israel?** (yes; Moses reminded them of God's blessings) **What blessings are listed here?** (food, good land which provides the food, houses, herds and flocks, silver and gold, manna) **What does the writer warn Israel about?** (forgetting just who gave them these blessings and becoming proud) **Can these instructions to Israel apply to us as a family too? How?** (we also must not become forgetful of praising God for what we have and not become proud in our self-sufficiency; we need to remember that *God* has provided all that we have) **And how specifically can we as a family not forget?** (we can list the things which He has so graciously given us and praise Him for these)

4. Place the bowl of "manna" next to the family candle. Give each family member another candle.

5. Announce that this bowl contains symbolic manna—reminders of blessings which God has given us. Ask everyone to light his or her individual candle from the family candle's flame and then take turns taking one piece of "manna" at a time. Every time a piece of manna is taken, that person is to share a specific blessing for which he or she is thankful. You may want to do as the writer

of Deuteronomy did and concentrate on your family's history of special blessings from God. Continue until the bowl is empty (or longer!) or until no one can think of any more blessings.

6. You may want to then sing "Thank You, Lord" before ending with a prayer of thanks to God.

SUGGESTIONS:

The box full of Styrofoam packing pressed at my imagination — wasn't this something like I had always envisioned manna to be? And hadn't we just bought a new *used* car (instead of the new one we all really wanted) that pointed out our need to practice *not forgetting* by *remembering* to thank our God for the blessing of *any* working car? (Our faithful old Subaru had just been hauled off by a junk dealer!)

If I'd had any concerns about the guys finding enough to be thankful for, these were quickly put to rest; we emptied the bowl in no time and probably could have gone through many more. And it's always a blessing — and sometimes revealing — to hear just what our guys are thankful for. Maybe this tradition would be worth repeating every Thanksgiving.

One final note — our new (used) car came from dear friends with the last name of *Gann*. And since we always give our cars a name, we dedicated the car that same evening — cleverly titling it forever "The Ganna Manna"!

NEW YEAR'S EVE: PAST AND FUTURE GOALS

MATERIALS NEEDED:

- ☐ a small cross (preferably a rough wooden one, but you could also use a cross from a necklace, wall plaque)
- ☐ a box (you will wrap the cross in this)
- ☐ wrapping paper (preferably gold or silver foil) and ribbon
- ☐ Scotch Tape
- ☐ scissors
- ☐ family candle and matches
- ☐ individual candles for each family member (if desired)
- ☐ Bible
- ☐ 3" x 5" file cards
- ☐ pens or pencils

TEXTS: Philippians 4:4-13 (or your family verses for this past year)

PREPARATION:

☐ Put your cross in the box and wrap it with foil paper and ribbon; you will want this package to look beautiful.

☐ Set aside the package, candles, matches, file cards, pens or pencils (one for each family member), and Bible for later.

☐ If your family has already chosen a passage to memorize for this current year, then substitute those verses for Philippians 4:4-13. (You may want to consider memorizing these verses—or a portion of them—for the *next* year, however.)

☐ Think through these questions, attempting to discover answers for children who may need assistance with them.

- What kind of year has this been for me spiritually?
- What have I learned?
- What was the hardest lesson?
- Because of this year, what are some areas needing growth in my life?

FAMILY TIME:

1. After putting the family candle at the center of the table and lighting it, begin your worship time with prayer.

2. If your children are old enough, give each one a smaller candle to hold. Tell your family that you will light these later from the family candle's flame.

3. Ask these questions, allowing family members to share after each one. (If someone does not have an answer, you may want to supply some suggestions. However, do not *require* any child to share.)

- **What kind of year has this been for me spiritually?**
- **What have I learned?**
- **What was the hardest lesson?**
- **Because of this year, what are some areas needing growth in my life?**

4. If your family members listed goals at last year's New Year's Eve celebration, discuss these now. You may want to ask questions like these: **Did I reach my goals? Why or why not? What can we do to encourage one another to meet our goals during this coming year?'**

5. Announce that before we decide on spiritual goals for this coming year, we need to discuss this special present. (Put the package on the table. Hopefully the shiny foil will reflect the candle's flame—making it appear even more beautiful.) You may want to then say something like this: **This beautiful package contains the greatest gift that was ever given. Can you guess what is inside?** After your children have given several guesses, allow them to open the package together—with your supervision and help. (NOTE: Use discretion here; if allowing your children to help will cause a distraction or possible problem, have a parent do this instead.) Pass the cross around the table, allowing everyone to hold it. You may want to ask questions like these:

- **Why is a cross the greatest gift that was ever given? What does it represent?** (the cross represents Jesus Christ—and that He died on the cross for our sins)
- **What else does that cross represent?** (that Christ overcame death; He arose from the grave!)
- **And how exactly are Christ's death and resurrection a gift to each one of us?** (when we seek repentance and ask Jesus Christ to become Lord of our lives, He gives us the gift of eternal life with Him!)

6. Announce that Christ's greatest gift of His very life and other continual blessings prompt us to want to give gifts also—of *ourselves.* Ask these questions: **What goal—what gift of *myself*—do I want to give to God this coming year? What can I do to grow spiritually and serve Him better?** As family members share, have them light their candles from the family candle's flame.

7. If your family memorized verses for this year, repeat them together now. If not, then have one parent read Philippians 4:4-13.

8. As a family, choose a portion of Scripture to memorize in the coming year. You may want to consider choosing the Philippians passage, a psalm, portions from Isaiah or other New Testament passages.

9. Close with prayer, taking turns thanking God for the past year's blessings and the new year's goals.

SUGGESTIONS:

Because the sharing questions do require conceptual abilities, this devotion is designed for children ages eight and older. However, if your children's ages vary—maybe you have two older and two younger ones—you can still use this devotion by helping smaller ones with their answers. And besides, I imagine that they would be fascinated with the candle, beautiful present, and the various activities. Just be sure to keep the length of your worship time appropriate for shorter attention spans.

Please do choose family verses for memorization! Our family has enjoyed this tradition tremendously, and there is a great sense of accomplishment for all of us when we've learned a portion of Scripture. We've memorized verses from Isaiah (chapter 40), Psalms, and the Philippians passage. And again, if you have little ones, they can also memorize Scripture—even if they learn only one verse or just a few words!

"YOU ARE THE LIGHT OF THE WORLD"

MATERIALS NEEDED:

- ☐ oil lamp complete with wick, oil, and matches
- ☐ scissors (a very sharp pair is helpful)
- ☐ pictures of oil lamps from New Testament times (We used *The Victor Handbook of Bible Knowledge*; bibliographical information is in the Recommended Resources section.)
- ☐ Bibles
- ☐ 3" x 5" file cards
- ☐ Scotch Tape
- ☐ pens and pencils
- ☐ felt-tip pens

TEXT: Matthew 5:13-16

PREPARATION:

☐ Check the oil lamp to make sure that it lights and burns correctly.

☐ Draw an oil lamp shape onto a 3" x 5" file card. After cutting out this oil lamp, trace enough for each family member plus one extra. (NOTE: I always make an extra in case one gets lost, someone needs another, etc.) Cut out these oil lamps.

☐ Study the Scripture passage. Review the background of this portion (preached by Jesus and entitled the Sermon on the Mount; this chapter also contains the Beatitudes) and then concentrate on verses 13-16 in particular. Consulting a book such as *The Victor Handbook of Bible Knowledge*, find and mark pages which contain pictures of oil lamps from New Testament times.

☐ Think through specific areas in which your children need to change in order for others to note the resulting change and praise God. (NOTE: Only offer these suggestions during your worship time if your children cannot think up areas on their own. Also, you may be tempted to do this devotion with very young children, adding the song "This Little Light of Mine" for further illustration. However, generally only children ages nine and up can grasp these conceptually mature ideas.)

☐ Construct a table marker, writing out Matthew 5:13-16.

☐ Set aside the oil lamp and matches, scissors, resource book, oil lamp shapes, and pens or pencils for later.

FAMILY TIME:

1. During dinner, discuss the background of Matthew 5. You may want to ask questions like:

- **What well-known sermon is in chapters 5, 6, and 7 of Matthew?** (the Sermon on the Mount)
- **Who preached the sermon?** (Jesus)
- **Why is it entitled this?** (Jesus spoke on a mountainside)
- **What familiar list begins chapter 5?** (the Beatitudes — "Blessed are. . . .")
- **"What is another word for *blessed?*** (*happy,* though the Beatitudes describe more than mere emotion; they speak of eternal joy)

2. Later, begin your family worship with prayer. Ask one or more family members to read the Scripture passage.

3. Show family members the pictures of oil lamps, pointing out familiar shapes, where the oil was poured in, and where the wick was inserted.

4. Place the oil lamp and matches on the table. After lighting the wick, turn off other lights so that the oil lamp is the only light-giving source in the room. Read verses 14 and 15 again, putting emphasis upon *"YOU* are the light." Discuss the futility of putting a bowl over the only light in a room. (Remind your family of the smaller lamps of biblical times; they could easily be covered by a bowl.) You may want to ask questions such as:

- **Do you think a family living during the New Testament times would cover its only light source? What does Jesus say they do instead?** (make the most use of the lamp — by putting it on a stand so that it gives off as much light as possible)
- **To whom does it then give light?** (to everyone in the house)
- **What else does Jesus say cannot be hidden?** (a city on a hill) **Why is this?** (because its lights are up above the others — accentuating those lights)

5. After turning on another light, extinguish the oil lamp's

wick. Then, cut the wick into a different shape. (We experimented with wavy, sharply pointed, and *v*-shaped cuts.) Relight the
lamp and again turn off any other house lights. Discuss and experiment with the flame until you are ready to repeat the process
and cut the wick into a different shape again.

6. Read verse 16 by the lamp's light. Then ask questions like:

● **What does Jesus mean when He says, *"In the same way, let
your* light shine before men"?** ([italics added]; we as Christians are vessels like an oil lamp; we shine out God's light—His
love—to all those around us)

● **What is the reason that we are to be willing vessels to
shine out God's light?** (so that others will notice our good
deeds and therefore *praise God)*

● **Do we sometimes put "bowls" over our lights?** (yes, when
our lives are not what they should be)

● **What does the shape of the wick tell us about the "shape"
of our lives?** (our lives reveal what is happening inside; we can
change that "shape" by growing spiritually)

7. Give each family member an oil lamp shape and a pencil or

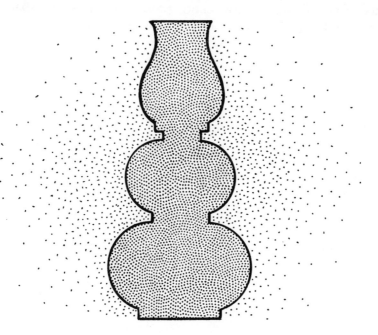

pen. After telling them that these lamps represent their lives, ask that they write down one thing that each one needs to change so that others will *see the change* and praise God.

8. End your worship time by exchanging the oil lamps; take turns praying for that person's desire to change.

SUGGESTIONS:

When a very dear friend gave us an oil lamp as a Christmas present, I recognized it immediately as a special gift. Not only would it always remind me of her sweet friendship, but I also realized it would become another treasured focal point for future family devotions. This family time was the first one we shared together around Carol's lamp.

The warm glow of the lamp provided a wonderful atmosphere for worship and the perfect visual object lesson that Jesus spoke of so long ago. Once again, the Master Teacher shows us that teaching—for *all* ages—is best taken in and applied (our sons' responses showed that they grasped the concept very well) when our senses respond to the key ideas. The clear memory of that flame still flickers in my mind, presenting an image that calls me—and hopefully our sons—to a lifestyle worthy of that glow.

Five
PRETEEN/TEEN AND PARENT – DEVELOPING THE INTIMATE RELATIONSHIP

DISCUSSION TIME: Reading *Preparing for Adolescence*

MATERIALS NEEDED:

☐ one or two copies of the book *Preparing for Adolescence* by Dr. James Dobson (Ventura, Calif.: Regal Books, 1978) NOTE: You may also wish to purchase the companion book entled *Preparing for Adolescence: Growth Guide* by Dr. Dobson. Consult the "Recommended Resources" section for pertinent information.

☐ questions for discussion from each chapter

PROCEDURE:

1. When your child is between the ages of nine to eleven (depending on emotional and physical maturity), secure one or two copies of this book. (NOTE: Having two is desirable in that you can then tell your child to jot notes or underline as he or she desires; this book can then be kept as the preteen's private copy.)

2. Read one chapter a week – child *and* parent(s) – planning a night (translation: put this on the calendar!) when you will then discuss the chapter together.

3. Set a tone for your discussion time that is relaxed, open, and nonthreatening. You may want to use these questions, make up your own, or use a combination of the two:

CHAPTER ONE
● What does Dr. Dobson mean by *inferiority?*
● Have you noticed the ways your classmates hide their inferi-

or feelings? What are some of these? Which ones do you tend to use?

- What strengths do you have that can compensate for your weaknesses? (Use this as a time to encourage your child.)
- Who are your *genuine* friends? How can you make real friends?
- What qualities does the world tend to value? What qualities does *God* value?

CHAPTER TWO

- What does the word *conformity* mean? Does it only relate to preteens and teens?
- What is the importance of having friends in relation to conformity?
- What fears have you experienced that caused you to conform?
- When is conforming *wrong?*
- Suppose that some classmates have drugs. What are you going to do? What part does being a courageous leader play?
- Can you think of someone who obviously feels inadequate or inferior and therefore needs your understanding? What specifically can you do to help this person?
- What does Dr. Dobson say is *God's* view of conformity?

CHAPTER THREE

- Do you have any specific questions about your body as it is right now? As it will be in the near future?
- What happens to a girl when she goes through puberty? A boy?
- What are the two most important things you must do to help your physical body as it goes through puberty?
- Does everyone go through puberty at *exactly the same time?* Should we then compare our development with others? Who sets the "time clock"?
- Who created sex and the desire for it? However, what limits does God place on having sex?
- What are some reasons for abstaining from sex until marriage?

- TO GIRLS: Do you have any concerns/fears about menstruation? (Reassure your daughter that you will always be available for these questions or concerns.)
- TO BOYS: Do you have any questions concerning "wet dreams"? (Reassure your son that he need not feel embarrassed when this happens.)
- TO GIRLS AND BOYS: In junior high you will need to undress for gym; to feel uncomfortable in front of your peers at these times is normal, but do you have any fears concerning this that you would like to discuss? (Again, encourage him or her to come to you in the future with any fears or problems in respect to this time.)

CHAPTER FOUR
- How did you do on the quiz? Were there any answers that you disagreed with?
- What is *infatuation*? How is it different from love?
- What is the true definition of love?

CHAPTER FIVE
- What happens to our emotions during the teen years?
- What are cyclical emotions? Can you give an example of when this happened to you?
- Why should we not make instant decisions based on our emotions?
- What are the steps to discerning or knowing God's will?
- What normal tensions and conflict will parents and teens face during these years? What do you think *we* will face?
- Is it wrong for you to question your Christian beliefs during these years? How can this be helpful?
- Can you think of someone with whom you like to identify?

CHAPTER SIX
- If you could write Dr. Dobson a question, what would it be?
- If you could ask me (us) any question, what would it be? (Note: You may want to ask your preteen to write down any questions. This way he or she may feel freer to ask difficult ones.)

SUGGESTIONS:

Reading this book with your preteen can be a most valuable experience in that it affords time for honest and open communication, relationship-building and self-image boosting at a crucial time in the child's life. I think one of the most important statements you're making to a son or daughter is, *"I care about you"*—enough to put personal time and attention into reading and discussing this book with you and you *alone.*

This approach also gives us parents the forum for the dreaded "sex talk"! Our kids *definitely* need to hear this information from Christian parents with a Christian worldview; please don't leave this duty to the public school system, your child's misinformed friends, or even a youth pastor. If we parents have not been open enough to talk honestly about sex with our young children, how will they ever be able to come to us as older teens when they most definitely will need our guidance concerning their sexual lives?

No, this exercise gives no "guarantees" whatsoever for a smooth adolescence; no activity can promise that. But hopefully this will be a beginning—a beginning for setting a pattern of communication between parent and teen during those years when openness—and accessibility on the parent's part—is an absolute must.

DEVELOPING PERSONAL GOALS

MATERIALS NEEDED:
- ☐ notebook paper
- ☐ pen or pencil
- ☐ Bible

ACTIVITIES FOR APPLICATION:
- sports–interscholastic, intramural, or park district
- entering junior or senior high school
- beginning various school activities: new classes, band, choir, student council, cheerleading, newspaper or yearbook, office staff helper, various clubs, etc.

PROCEDURE:

1. When your child is about to begin a new activity—and *especially* if he or she appears hesitant, unsure, fearful, or has had past problems with this particular activity—ask him or her to compose a list of personal goals. CAUTION! *Don't make this sound like just another homework assignment!* Instead, approach this idea with excitement and a note of encouragement, reassuring your child that this list need not be extensive nor "homework neat." Emphasize that this activity will be of great benefit, allowing him or her to direct energies in specific ways that will greatly help achieve a beneficial activity—for the child *and* parent. (In other words, stress that this will greatly aid you also as a parent!)

2. Encourage your child to spend some time in prayer first. Then, explain that these goals are *not* related to abilities or "output" but instead are associated with *character-building.* For example, if your child is entering a competitive sports activity, one of his or her goals should *not* be "to score 10 points per game." Instead, an example of a character-building goal might be to "not give up even when losing" or to "not make fun of someone who makes an error." If your child is beginning a new class, a goal should *not* be to make an *A;* instead, he or she may write down "I will attempt to be responsible and turn in every homework assignment on time." Be sure to give several specific examples so

that your child understands what is being asked of him or her. Finally, you may want to suggest areas which the child might want to address. For example, if he or she has demonstrated a problem in the past in getting along with others in a group, you may want to ask your child to consider ways to confront this.

3. You may also want to ask your child to select a verse to accompany his or her goals. (You might want to memorize it together too.) If the child needs help in choosing an appropriate verse, help him or her consult a concordance to find one.

4. Set a reasonable date (not too short, thus not giving enough time—not too long, allowing procrastination) for the goals to be done. Put this time on the calendar so that you may plan to discuss and pray over these goals together.

5. When you are ready to discuss the goals, pick a relaxed setting in your home in which to do so. Ask your son or daughter to read the list aloud. You may want to suggest additions or revisions, but do so cautiously and gently. *It is imperative that these remain the child's goals; true ownership is an essential element!* Remember, parents, that you are not enforcing a list of *your* desires for your child; instead, these must be the *child's* goals for personal growth.

6. Ask your son or daughter to sign and date the list. Then, you as parents may want to also sign after writing out a pledge something like this: "I promise to support, encourage, and pray for you in striving to reach these goals." (NOTE: You may want to merely suggest your signing the list at first. If your child balks at the suggestion, do not force the issue.)

7. Pray for your child, asking God to help him or her have the wisdom, strength, and courage to strive to meet these goals. Thank God for his or her willingness to attempt them and ask that this may be a learning experience for all of you.

8. Ask your child if he or she prefers to keep the list in his possession or post it in a prominent place—such as the refrigerator. (Pluses for the refrigerator are that there is less possibility of its being lost and its prominence reminds parent and child to pray and continually work on the goals.)

9. As your son or daughter heads out the door to go to this particular activity, gently remind him or her of the goals. You may

want to ask questions like: **How are you doing? Have you noticed improvement in any particular areas? Are some giving
you trouble? How can I pray more specifically?** And continually remind your child of this: **I am praying for you!** Then, be sure
to follow through with that promise.

10. When the activity comes to an end, spend some time evaluating achievement, growth, and room for improvement in relation
to these goals. *Don't make this a critical time!* Instead, use this
discussion for encouragement—recognizing the child's attempts
and pointing out the areas needing improvement and thus possible future goals. End this time with prayer, thanking God for
character qualities that have been enhanced and asking Him to
help your child develop even more in the future.

SUGGESTIONS:

Intense competitiveness comes naturally to our guys. And unfortunately, I can't blame all those inherited genes on just my
husband! So why have I always approached each new season of
sports activities with the unrealistic expectation that this year, this
time, this team, this *child* will be entirely different—and that
competitive drive will be maturely under control? I guess finally
my expectations hit against the reality in a way that said, "So do
something constructive about this! Get a tool—for you *and* your
child!" The result, our personal goals list, has *not* been the solu-
tion that ended all problems. It *has* become an invaluable tool
that helps our sons and us as parents work in a specific, constructive, personally accountable way toward making life-changing
improvements.

I want to emphasize how much this has helped *me* as a frustrated parent. So often I found myself nagging and offering pieces of
advice here and there. This tool gave me *specifics* to pray for—in
areas which the guys *themselves* recognized they wanted and
needed to improve.

Our discussions were not a "I'll lecture while you listen" sort of
communication either. Instead, *ownership* was a key element.
Craig learned this important lesson when he was a youth pastor:
what the kids *owned* they always tended to work harder at, put
more effort into, and feel more personal responsibility for. If

something became "Pastor Craig's idea," it just wasn't met with the same input at all. I think you'll find this same response in regard to these personal goals. If you compose them *for* your child, they'll merely be *your* goals; if your child writes them, they will be *owned* by the child. And what is owned has a greater opportunity to be *changed.*

PREPARING TO DATE: WRITING STANDARDS

MATERIALS NEEDED:
- ☐ notebook paper
- ☐ pen or pencil
- ☐ Bible

APPLICATION:
- to use before your child begins dating in an informal group, "double" dating, or "single" dating

PROCEDURE:

1. As soon as your child shows an interest in dating, tell him or her that you require a *written list* of dating standards before he or she may go out on a first date. (NOTE: You as parents must determine exactly what constitutes a date from the three types listed above—group, double, or single. Some of you may want to require a standards list before *any* type of date; others may ask for one before a double or a single date. Be sure to discuss this as parents before the issue arises with your teen. A "united front" is an essential element!)

2. Inform your teen that this will indeed be his or her standards; you parents will not be the authors! Again, child *ownership* is an important factor here. A list of rules not owned by a teen will have little impact on his or her habits or lifestyle.

3. Parents, you will need to be very specific concerning the areas and issues which your teen will need to address; therefore, discuss these points beforehand so that you can list these areas for your preteen or teenager. (You may want to pray about these areas yourselves before you discuss them with your son or daughter.) Areas that we told our son to address were:
- Do I plan to date any non-Christians, only Christians, or only *growing* Christians?
- What places will I take a date? Youth activities? Movies? Dances? Bowling alleys? Homes for parties?
- Are there some places which I know I should avoid? Trouble spots at school? Parking lots? Parties in homes of unsaved acquaintances? Being in a car alone?

- If I do attend movies, which ones are acceptable? Which ones are unacceptable? How will I judge this?
- Will I agree to inform my parents of where I will be and any changes in plans that may occur during the date?
- What is a reasonable curfew for a school night? For the weekend? Am I willing to be flexible concerning curfews when I am extremely busy, feeling stressed, or sick?
- If some unforeseen event or emergency occurs and I will not be able to make my curfew, will I agree to call home immediately? If, however, I am late simply because I am tardy, what do I believe is a reasonable consequence?
- If I am out late on a Saturday night, will I still attend church?
- Where will I draw the line as to what is considered acceptable behavior? Kissing? Heavy kissing? Petting? Sex?
- What do I consider a fair amount of time to have the car? How will I request to use the car? Will I recognize the supreme importance of driving safely?
- How do I plan to show that I am a responsible and maturing teen in relation to my dating lifestyle?
- If I am a Christian, how does my commitment to God and my testimony to others affect my dating lifestyle?

After reading our list, you will want to edit and add to these questions to make a list that fits your preteen or teenager. (You will also need to take into account the age at which you have your son or daughter do this. If he or she is younger, guidelines concerning the car, for example, will not be applicable. Therefore, you will need to have your teen address this when the time is appropriate.)

4. After giving your teen the questions he or she must address, you may also want to ask about deciding on a Scripture verse especially for this occasion in his or her life. Your teen may want to pick a favorite verse to be used as a type of "dedication passage," or he or she may have a life verse which could be repeated at this special time. Allow your teen to choose.

5. Give your son or daughter a reasonable amount of time to complete the standards list, encouraging him or her to spend a good deal of time in prayer during this process. Point out that the list MUST BE DONE before he or she will be allowed to go on a

date! Assure your teen that *you* as parents will be praying also.

6. When your teen has completed the list, you will want to take time to discuss it together. There are several ways to do this: meet informally at home, plan a special night out for both parents or a single parent and teen to discuss this over a meal, or have only the parent of the same sex take the teen to a restaurant for a one-on-one discussion. (Note: If you are a single parent of a teen of the opposite sex, you may want to ask a godly trusted friend with whom your teen feels comfortable and accepted to take your teen to dinner.) Some parents make this into an important commitment time, giving the teen a gift as a symbol of the son's or daughter's pledge. Whatever you judge fits your teen's personality the best, do plan and take time to discuss the standards list with your teen. Your time and attention communicates to the teen that *this is important to you.*

7. Discuss the Scripture verse with your teen also, asking for and pointing out ways this applies to his or her Christian lifestyle.

8. End your time together in prayer. Be sure to ask God to help your teen be wise whenever he or she must make decisions and to keep your teen pure spiritually, emotionally, and physically as he or she enters this most exciting time of life.

SUGGESTIONS:

A child's *ownership* is again extremely important. We told our son that the standards were necessary for our permission to date and that he must address certain issues, but *he* composed his list. I judge that he does feel ownership for the guidelines and therefore also feels responsibility for abiding by them.

Certainly there will be areas of disagreement over what *you* consider appropriate and what your *teen* judges to be acceptable, but as you discuss and negotiate for agreement, do attempt to keep an attitude of more equal discussion and compromise. If your tone clearly comes across as "I am the parent and you will do what I say," I judge that the list will be nearly meaningless. We have found teens to be quite willing to negotiate and compromise — but only when they have been given a forum to have their say and when they have been made to feel an important part of the decision-making process.

Lastly, I think all of us Christian parents would agree that the most important part of the entire process is *prayer:* while your teen makes the list, before he or she even begins to date, while on a date, and throughout this extremely important part of his or her life. And the next most important part is to *let your teen KNOW that you are praying!* Remind him, let him see you on your knees, and let him hear your pleas; I don't know of a better way to show your love for your teen!

PARENT AND PRETEEN/TEEN CAMPING TRIP

MATERIALS NEEDED:

- ☐ planning and time for a camping trip with your preteen or teenager (You may want to combine this with fishing, hiking, boating, touring historical sites, etc.—whatever you and your teen enjoy doing together.)
- ☐ equipment for camping: tent, sleeping bags, cooking utensils, food, clothes, personal accessories, sports equipment
- ☐ wood and matches for a campfire
- ☐ Bibles

APPLICATION:

    ● to use during influential times in your preteen's or teen's life: before entering junior or senior high school, when he or she seems open to your input and friendship or even when your teen does *not*—and is therefore somewhat rebellious and in need of time away with you

PROCEDURE:

1. With your teen's input and help, plan a trip together for at least two night's duration. Allow the teen to help decide: the nature of the trip (for example, exploring historical sites versus hiking), location, meals, etc.

2. Purchase supplies and then pack your car together. Every step of the process should hopefully be a *joint* effort.

3. During your trip, attempt to keep the atmosphere relaxed and friendly. Any intensity or pressure on your part as a parent with an *agenda* will most likely only "shut down" your teen. Also, if your teen has a permit, allow him or her to share driving time.

4. If possible, build a campfire every night. As both of you sit around the fire, staring into the flames, this may be the perfect time to communicate on a deeper level with your teenager. You may want to consider approaching your time together in these ways:

    a. Ask very open-ended questions such as **What's going on? What's happening in your life right now?** The key in this approach is to *actively listen* to your teen's answers. Your ability to skillfully probe those "hidden" replies—nonverbals (such as averted eyes, body movements which pull him or her away from you, or nervous, quick actions); feelings which come through the words (muffled, rushed, or strongly emotive answers); and hints at deeper problems or conflicts (for example, a reply such as "Nothin's goin' on since I'm obviously not the most popular girl in my class")—will determine your *next* question. Actively listen for the cues and clues that will hopefully guide you and your teen into the personalized conversation that he or she needs.

Once you can identify an area, you will need to further clarify by asking questions like, **What do you mean by that? Are you feeling** (for example, frustrated, lonely, rejected)? **I may have felt** (frustrated, lonely, rejected) **like you when** _____ (give an example of an experience when you felt this way). **Is that what you're feeling? Does my feeling seem to be like yours?** If your relatable example is off target, think of another and share again. *Your ability to share openly will often determine how much your teen is willing to then share with you.* Again, watch for the nonverbals that often send messages that are louder than words.

    b. Ask questions such as these:

- **Is there anything that I'm doing that is frustrating you?**
- **Is there anything that** (your dad, your mom) **is doing that is frustrating you?**
- **Is there anything that I'm *not* doing that you wish I *would* do?**

You may want to replace the word *frustrating* with other feelings such as hurting, embarrassing, angering, or alienating—to the point of rejection.

Then again, you must watch and listen for the signals which will tell you which direction your questions (and sharing) need to take. Use the process given above (under letter *a*) to bring out the feelings in this and related areas.

    c. Even before you have left for your trip, you should think through *key areas* which you believe you and your teen need to talk about and explore. Extremely important areas in a teen's life to consider are these: relationships with you, the parents, and with peers, teachers, boyfriend/girlfriend, siblings; scholastic and athletic abilities—and the closely resulting self-image; appearance and apparent acceptance by peers on this basis; and most importantly, his or her relationship with God. You may want to begin by asking, **How do you feel about** _____? Then, as in both *a* and *b* above, concentrate on getting at these feelings first with a combination of questioning and sharing.

Please note that the recurring theme that seems to run through all of these areas can be summed up in three words: acceptance or rejection. If a teen *feels* rejected, no matter what the actual facts may be and especially no matter what *you* the parent believe to be true, if your teen truly *feels* rejected, then this is truth to him or her. Arguing those feelings away will *not* solve the problem; instead, seek to identify with your teen, giving examples of when you felt rejected in this same area. Only then can you begin to work on your teen's feelings of rejection with the reassurances that God loves him or her *no matter what* and that *you* will love him or her *no matter what*. CAUTION: Don't ever attempt to say these words *unless you truly mean them!* Your teen can spot a phony response easily.

Above all, remember that this is *not* a "parent lecture" time. Instead, attempt to set a definite atmosphere of "parent to adult or friend" rather than "parent to child." Of course, this will depend on the age and maturity of your son or daughter, but keep in mind that your relationship is definitely in a process of change. Slowly and surely you must and need to move from a parent-child relationship to an adult-adult one. This camping trip can be an important time for you to set future patterns and reassure your teen that you will allow—and desire—for this change to occur.

5. You may want to spend time together in God's Word, but if your teen seems bored, put-off, or openly against this idea, I would not push it. Keep in mind this most important fact: good communication with your teen has at its base *relationship*—with you, with friends, with siblings, with teachers. And at the base of each of these relationships—giving support (or lack of), ability to build (or break down), and desire to grow creatively (or draw inward, shutting off the uniqueness and specialness that God has built into each of us)—is *relationship with God.* Do not think that, just because you are not working through a Scripture pas-

sage together on this trip, that you are not helping your teen to grow spiritually. Your interaction and demonstrated love can help your teen see that God's Word is truly alive and life changing in a way that he or she has never realized before.

6. Lastly, don't forget to have *fun*. Apply liberal amounts of laughter (and allow it at your expense if you can laugh too!) whenever possible!

SUGGESTIONS:

As a youth pastor, Craig was always amazed at how even the most quiet and withdrawn teens would suddenly open up when gathered around the warm and nonthreatening atmosphere of a campfire. We determined years ago that we would use this excellent tool to help us communicate with our children—and them with us.

When I asked Craig about the specific questions he would use when he was around the campfire, he basically responded with the three areas given above. However, note that, as Craig pointed out to me, he concentrated more on *technique* rather than specific questions. Your ability to *actively* listen (it's *not* a passive process because you must work to take note of nonverbals and hidden emotional responses) and then gently and skillfully probe into the needed areas will determine the depth of your communication.

One final word of caution: consider your expectations before you go. I suppose all of us as parents will probably have to admit to expectations that are far above what will be attained. But recognizing this fact and then attempting to adjust them should put things back into a better perspective. Lastly, remember that this should be viewed as a beginning—and building time. Whatever advances you make—or *don't* make—can hopefully be accepted as one step toward a better relationship. Even a tiny step puts one farther along the pathway.

Six
JUST FUN!

THE FAMILY CHRONICLES

MATERIALS NEEDED:

- [ ] access to typewriter and copier or computer and printer (NOTE: If necessary, you may write out your family chronicles in longhand.)
- [ ] notebook paper
- [ ] pen or pencil

PREPARATION:

- [ ] If all of your children are at a reading age and if you desire, make a copy of your family chronicles for each family member. (If some of your children are younger, you may want only one copy for a parent to read from.) You will want to title it "The (your last name here) Family Chronicles" and personalize it to fit your unique family personality. Ours went like this:

The Williford Family Chronicles

Once upon a time there was a family by the name of Williford. The Dad, Craig, had the nickname of _____. Mom, Carolyn, was called _____; the elder son, Robb, was _____ and the younger son, Jay, was called _____. Even their dog Bojangles had a nickname; it was _____.

Dad's favorite sport was _____, though he looked kind of _____ when he played. Mom enjoyed doing _____, but her legs always looked _____ when she ran. Robb loved to play _____ even though his face looked _____ whenever he won and Jay especially enjoyed _____ though his hair looked _____ after he finished. Bojangles just thought _____ was the best thing ever. And he always looked _____.

The whole Williford family enjoyed other unusual activities too. When no one was looking, Dad would _____. Mom thought she was better than anyone else at _____. Robb could run and _____ at the same time and Jay could _____ in his sleep, he was so good at it. Bojangles learned to _____ from watching Dad.

When someone or something surprised the Willifords, they did some strange things. Dad would _____ until he gained ten pounds and Mom would _____ until she drove her family crazy! When something surprised Robb, he would jump on top of the _____ for two or three days. Jay would generally wiggle his _____ until he _____ and fell down, exhausted. Whenever Bojangles was surprised, his tail could do some amazing things; it looked like a _____.

I must admit, those Willifords looked a bit different too. Dad's _____ was the biggest one I've ever seen. And Mom's _____ wasn't tiny either. Robb's _____ appeared to be connected to his nose and Jay's _____ looked just like a dinosaur's. Bojangles' _____ made every other dog in the neighborhood "howl" with laughter. (Great pun, eh?)

As you can tell, this is no normal family. In fact, the four words that best describe those Willifords are _____, _____, _____, and _____. And Bojangles is just plain _____!

THE END

Be sure to personalize yours however you wish!

☐ Make one copy of the corresponding word list. Again, depending on your children's ages, you will need to vary the instructions. If your children are old enough to understand verbs, nouns, and adjectives, you may want to use these terms; their English teachers will be delighted with this review! Smaller children can be asked to provide actions, more specific objects and "describers." Here's the list of words your family will need to provide:

1. nickname (you may want to suggest the names of the Seven Dwarves)

2. nickname
3. nickname
4. nickname
5. nickname
6. hobby or sport
7. adjective (or a "describer"; give some examples)
8. hobby or sport
9. adjective
10. hobby or sport
11. adjective
12. hobby or sport
13. adjective
14. hobby or sport
15. adjective
16. verb (or an activity)
17. verb (activity)
18. verb (activity)
19. verb (activity)
20. verb (activity)
21. verb (activity)
22. verb (activity)
23. piece of furniture
24. body part
25. verb (an action)
26. noun (something that is long and thin)
27. body part
28. body part
29. body part
30. body part
31. body part
32. adjective (describer)
33. adjective
34. adjective
35. adjective
36. adjective

☐ Set aside your chronicles, word list, and pen or pencil for later.

FAMILY TIME:

1. Begin with prayer, asking God to bless your fun time together this evening.

2. Take out your word list; announce that you need your family's help in completing an important story. You can proceed in two ways: either take turns, continually going from one family member to the next as they give answers or allow everyone to shout out possible answers as you write down the most "creative" (and funniest!) answer. Generally, older children can do the first suggestion and younger children can participate more easily by using the second. Proceed through the entire list of needed words, giving further explanations whenever necessary. Be sure to write your answers next to each space on the list with *legible* handwriting!

3. If you made copies of your chronicles for everyone, hand these out at this time. Then, slowly read your family's story, carefully putting the suggested words into their correct blanks and pausing for frequent laughter!

4. End with prayer, thanking God for the gift of laughter and the ability to experience fun within the family.

SUGGESTIONS:

I can remember doing this game as a child in grammar school and the hilarious results. Little did I know that the teacher was using this creative teaching tool to review our grammar skills; all I knew was that I thoroughly enjoyed the funny word combinations and pictured situations that resulted.

Please do be careful, however, that the fun does not become a cruel joke on a sensitive child. The parent who asks for the words should monitor them to be sure that no combination of words hits at another's sensitive areas. Also, a child who is going through a period of low self-esteem may be hurt further by this activity at that time.

As usual, our responses found that the laugh was on Mom. How come Dad's *brain* was "the biggest one ever seen" and "Mom thought she was better than anyone else when it came to *sitting*"? Never fails.

BOTTLE BALL

MATERIALS NEEDED:

☐ several empty two-liter plastic bottles
☐ an *old* tennis racket (You may want to watch for some of these at a garage or yard sale.)
☐ base markers

PREPARATION:

☐ Rinse out the empty 2-liter bottles; replace caps tightly.
☐ Position the base markers evenly in your backyard. (Or, you may want to play at a local park.)
☐ Set aside the bottles and tennis racket for later.

FAMILY TIME:

1. Announce that you will be playing a new game that is entitled "Bottle Ball." It is played like baseball except that it has just a few different twists: you will use an old tennis racket instead of a bat and your balls will be empty two-liter bottles. Explain that you will need several "balls" because the bottles generally get battered and broken pretty quickly!

2. Divide into teams, making them as evenly matched as possible. Take turns pitching and playing outfield. If your family is smaller like ours, you may want to use our rules for two-member teams: (1) If the outfield catches the bottle, as in baseball, it is an automatic out; (2) If the outfielder returns the bottle to the pitcher *before the batter reaches first base,* then the batter is out; (3) If the runner does not make it home on his or her teammate's hit, then this runner bats again as the teammate advances to the farthest gained base; (4) Continue exchanging places as necessary until the opposing team forces three outs.

3. Continue playing as many innings as desired or until you run out of bottles!

SUGGESTIONS:

I guess the type of creativity that thinks up new ways to use old objects runs in our family, for my *sons* invented this game! Craig and I had listened to them giggle, cackle, and laugh the entire time they played Bottle Ball. We'd wonder, "What on earth makes this game that much fun?" Whenever the guys had friends over, they'd introduce *them* to this new game too; pretty soon I heard the friends' parents complaining that "Now we have to buy two-liter bottles instead of canned pop. Our kids insist we must have the bottles to play something called Bottle Ball!"

So, after a few "Come on; you'll love it!"'s Craig and I were coaxed into our first game of Bottle Ball. I don't know if the fun derives from *whapping* that bottle (the sound it makes is wonderful!), from continuing to wreck an already hopeless tennis racket (who plays tennis like Chris Evert anyway?), from destroying what was destined for the trash can (get out those pent-up frustrations!), from the resulting terrific batting averages (you can't easily miss hitting a bottle with a tennis racket) or from playing an obviously ridiculous-looking game—and enjoying every minute of it!

Thanks, Robb and Jay! Bottle Ball is one creative, resourceful, and hilarious game!

CRAZY BALLOON BIBLE DRILL RELAY

MATERIALS NEEDED:
- ☐ balloons (5" diameter works well)
- ☐ poster board (two pieces or more) or a large cardboard box
- ☐ felt-tip pens
- ☐ stapler and staples
- ☐ notebook paper
- ☐ scissors
- ☐ pen or pencil
- ☐ Scotch Tape
- ☐ long, thin pieces of cloth for tying wrists together— possibly scarves (You will need enough to tie family members' wrists; the number of ties needed will depend on whether you divide into two or more teams.)
- ☐ Bibles
- ☐ various accessories for the game (crackers, toothpaste and toothbrushes, cups, ice cream bars, or whatever creative additions you decide to use)
- ☐ pins (for popping the balloons)
- ☐ one copy of the instructions for the game

TEXTS: We used these verses for the Bible drill
   Jeremiah 31:29
   Isaiah 5:22
   Psalm 19:10
   1 Timothy 5:10
   Ruth 4:7
   2 Thessalonians 3:10
   Luke 12:22

PREPARATION:

   ☐ Decide how you will divide your family into teams. Because we have four in our family, we divided into two teams and tied together Craig and Robb and then Jay and me. If your family is made up of more than four, you may want to consider tying more than just two people together (three joined at the same

wrist would be rather interesting!) or forming more teams. If you do decide on more than two teams, then you will need to make additional game boards.

☐ Write out a list of rules for the game such as:

a. The name of this game is the "Crazy Balloon Bible Drill Relay!" Each team's object is to complete all seven Bible drills and activities as quickly as possible—while being *tied at the wrist to your teammate!*

b. You must proceed in order through numbers 1–7.

c. First, pop the balloon with the pin.

d. Second, read the Bible reference; one person looks up the verse while the other reads it aloud. (FOR EACH OF THE RE-MAINING REFERENCES, ALTERNATE WHO LOCATES THE VERSE AND WHO READS IT.)

e. Third, read the instructions underneath the reference. Whatever the directions say to do, remember that DAD DOES THIS FOR ROBB, AND THEN ROBB DOES THIS FOR DAD. For example, if the instructions were to say, "Brush your hair," then Dad would brush Robb's hair and then Robb would brush Dad's hair. (Likewise, Jay does this for Mom and Mom does this for Jay.) YOU MAY NOT HELP YOUR TEAMMATE COMPLETE HIS OR HER ACTIVITY!! Also, your teammate must always use *your* hygienic or beauty articles and you must use *his* or *hers.* Therefore, Dad and Robb must go downstairs for Dad to get Robb's hairbrush to use on Robb's hair; Dad and Robb must then go upstairs for Robb to get Dad's hairbrush to brush Dad's hair. REMEMBER THAT YOU WILL ALWAYS BE TIED AT THE WRISTS TOO! (This adds just a bit more of a challenge!)

f. When you have both completed your required activity, go back to your game board to pop the next balloon, read your Bible drill and discover your *next* activity. Proceed through all seven balloons.

g. Though both teams' lists contain the same instructions, these activities are NOT given in the same order. Therefore, the teams will be completing activities at different times to hopefully avoid collisions!

h. Are there any questions? If not, then teammates tie those wrists together and begin!

You will want to refine, change, and fit these rules for your family's size, children's ages, and abilities. Just be creative and have fun!

☐ Construct the game boards; you will need to make one for each team. You may want to cut up a cardboard box so that the finished boards sit upright. (If you're using poster board, you'll need to construct bases so that the boards can stand alone.) At the top of each game board with a bright-colored felt-tip pen write: "Crazy Balloon Bible Drill Relay!" For two teams, you will need to blow up fourteen balloons. (Keep in mind that the boards will need to be big enough to staple seven blown-up balloons on each one.)

Next, cut the notebook paper into 28 smaller pieces (for two teams) approximately 4″ square. For each team you'll need to write out the seven Bible drill verses on separate sheets of paper; then write out the required activities on seven other sheets. The corresponding verses and activities that we used were:

- Brush your teeth — Jeremiah 31:29
- Comb your hair — Psalm 19:10
- Change a sock — 1 Timothy 5:10
- Eat a piece of cracker — Luke 12:22
- Change a shoe — Ruth 4:7
- Drink ½ cup water — Isaiah 5:22
- Eat an ice cream bar — 2 Thessalonians 3:10

(As stated in the list of rules, I changed the order of the activities for the other team except for the ice cream bar; this was the last instruction for both teams.) Be sure to number the reference and activity after writing them on sheets of paper to avoid confusion.

For each numbered activity, tape first the directions for the activity (folded over once) to the game board, tape the Bible verse (also folded over) on top of this and then lastly, staple the end of the blown-up balloon over the top so that the balloon covers the two sheets of paper. Repeat this for all seven activities, spacing them so that there will be enough room for the balloons. Be sure to make a game board for each team.

☐ Set aside the completed game boards, pins, instructions, Bibles, wrist ties, cups, and instructions for later.

FAMILY TIME:

1. Begin with prayer, thanking God for an evening to have fun together.

2. Announce the name of this evening's game and then read the list of instructions. Be sure that everyone understands the rules and the intent of the activities. (NOTE: You may want to vary which wrists you tie together based on whether family members are left- or right-handed. And depending on the ages of your children, you may want to make the game easier—or more difficult!)

3. Enjoy the hilarious—and rather awkward!—activities together. As you end by "feeding" each other the ice cream bars, discuss the most difficult, awkward, and humorous situations.

4. End with prayer, thanking God for your family.

SUGGESTIONS:

Often I'm amazed at the ideas that pop into my head. (Where do they come from?) This idea came one evening just before I drifted off to sleep—and then I lay giggling to myself in anticipation of the fun that it promised to be!

It is an incredibly awkward experience to attempt to brush another's teeth or change someone else's shoe—especially with one wrist tied and high-top sneakers that have mile-long laces tangled through 100 eyes. And did we ever make a mess with those ice cream bars! (Craig suggested that it would have been even more fun to feed each other cake; you may want to attempt that one.) Our dog joined in again too—barking, running up and down steps, and generally being in the way at every step.

This family time was definitely a hit—the guys loved it and we had a great time together. But one quick word of warning, parents: ONLY ATTEMPT THIS ONE WHEN YOU HAVE PLENTY OF ENERGY!

AGGRAVATION CHARADES

MATERIALS NEEDED:
☐ props for skits

PREPARATION:
☐ Decide how to divide your family into two teams. Then, think of several suggestions for your game of charades. Choose family situations which you can act out that frustrate, aggravate, or annoy one or more family members. CAUTION: Be careful that you do not choose situations which can be hurtful, cause anger, or single out one person in a damaging manner. The purpose of this family time is to see the humor in situations which really do not have great importance or significance. By focusing on the humorous side of things which aggravate us, hopefully we can learn to laugh—rather than grump!—about these same or similar situations in the future.

☐ To stimulate your thinking, here are some of the situations which our family considered:

a. Our dog gets extremely excited when he hears one of us say, "Walk!" (Translation: he goes absolutely bananas.) *I* happen to think it's fun to get Bojangles all excited before Robb takes him for a walk; for some unknown reason, Robb does not find this amusing at all. This skit was Robb's choice for something that aggravates him.

b. When Craig comes home from playing a couple hours of basketball with "the boys" (translation: men who *play* like boys and sincerely regret it the next morning), he tosses his sweaty gym clothes (whew!) on the steps to the basement; they sit there until he finishes taking a shower. This is one of Jay's pet peeves and therefore was his choice for charades.

c. While watching television, Jay has the habit of taking off shoes, socks, and often a sweater or shirt—dropping each casually on the floor of the family room. This is not Mom's favorite scenario. (Translation: this drives *her* bananas.) I chose this skit for aggravation charades. (NOTE: See "Nagging Eliminator: 'Contract' " for help with this aggravation!)

d. Being a typical teenager who is very possessive concerning his "territory," Robb gets a bit uptight when someone steps into his room (translation: far enough to emit one breath of air) without his express permission. This can be a bit unnerving for Dad, who still keeps trying to convince us we live under his "dictatorship"; therefore, Craig chose this situation to act out.

I hope these examples give you some ideas for skits for your family. Again, note that each one pokes fun in a nonthreatening manner and hopefully elicits grins and laughter—during the skit and in the future when the "aggravation" may occur again!

FAMILY TIME:

1. Begin with prayer, asking God to use laughter to help family members learn about each other and themselves.

2. Divide into two teams. The number on each team should be as equal as possible, and the more children in your family, the better the creative input!

3. Explain that you will be playing "Aggravation Charades!"—a game in which two teams take turns acting out skits for the other team to guess what occasion is being presented. Describe the skits as "situations within our family which have produced aggravation and frustration for one or more family members." Point out that these are *not* to be embarrassing, hurtful, or angering circumstances for any member of the family. Finally, add that the goal is to laugh together at our various pet peeves and humorous habits.

4. After assigning separate rooms for secrecy, direct each team to decide on situations, collect needed props, and rehearse several skits. (Feel free to do as many as each team wishes.)

5. When each team is ready, take turns acting out and guessing skits. (NOTE: Though the situations being acted out were generally recognizable right away, we withheld our guesses until the presenting team had finished its skit. That way, we all enjoyed laughing at the occasion *and* the actors!)

6. If your children seem open to the possibility, suggest having a short discussion time concerning some of the situations—and maybe others that come to mind. This may be an excellent time to vent those frustrations and pet peeves, allowing time for further elaboration.

7. End with prayer, holding hands as a family.

SUGGESTIONS:

This exercise was a healthy one for us — providing a relaxed and even fun forum to air aggravations that can sometimes simmer into full conflict. Somehow that added humor often helps to tone down our more frustrated responses to family members too; by looking at ourselves through the eyes of laughter, we seem to take ourselves less seriously. And then maybe what once elicited growls can now bring a chuckle. Or at least a grin *after* the glare!

"WILLIFORDY!"

MATERIALS NEEDED:

- ☐ poster board (You'll probably want to make a base to allow it to sit upright also.)
- ☐ one package of 3″ square self-stick papers
- ☐ ruler
- ☐ pens and pencils
- ☐ felt-tip pens (bright colors)
- ☐ bell (NOT a delicate one!)
- ☐ notebook paper
- ☐ piano or keyboard
- ☐ 3″ x 5″ cards

PREPARATION:

☐ Decide on the four subjects you will use for your game of "Willifordy!" (or "Smithardy!" or "Jonesardy!"—whatever your last name happens to be) Because we were celebrating one year in a new home, our subjects related to this. After deciding on the subjects which relate to your family's interests and activities, you must then choose five questions (for each subject) and the corresponding answers.

☐ Prepare poster board by first writing your name at the top (add *ardy!* to the end to imitate the television game show "Jeopardy") with a felt-tip pen. Then, using a ruler and a pencil, measure and mark off four vertical columns and five horizontal columns. (This should then make a total of 20 squares for your answers.) Label the top vertical columns as you desire; our subjects were *Project Parts, Special Visits, Answers to Prayer—Name the Need,* and *Best of Times.* Then, just under the subject titles, write the point value *100;* continue down each square, assigning point values up to *500.* (Write these numbers at the *top* of each square.) You should then have all four vertical columns labeled with point values from 100 to 500.

☐ On notebook paper, write out your ideas for questions and answers for each subject. Then, assign point totals for each, attempting to make the difficulty of the questions rise with the points earned for a correct answer. You will then need to copy all

of your answers and questions in each category (in correct order) on a different piece of notebook paper. To help you with creative ideas for your family, these are the answers and questions I used for our game:

Project Parts

100 - saw, paneling, nails
"What is paneling the family room?"

200 - brushes, rags, can, widgets, ladders
"What is painting outside?"

300 - tiles, grout, cabinet
"What is a new medicine cabinet and tiling?"

400 - brushes, rags, rollers, pans, cans
"What is painting inside?"

500 - saw, hatchet, rakes, shovels
"What is removing the old shrubs?"

Special Visits

100 - Huh-Huh, Ruth, Grandma Barclay, Glenn, Donna, Aunt Marilyn
"What is Cleveland?"

200 - dinosaurs, Egyptian tombs, Eskimos
"What is the Field Museum?"

300 - inner tubes, snow, Ping-Pong
"What is the cabin?"

400 - white buildings, military, Dale and Kim
"What is the Citadel?"

500 - sand, waves, surfing
"What is Emerald Isle?"

Answers to Prayer—Name the Need

100 - silver, uses a key, borrowed
"What is a car?"

200 - paper-printer, book-writer, homework-helper
"What is a computer?"

300 - traveling home, friend-visitor, relaxer
"What is the Gann's motorhome?"

400 - black, gas-powered, food fixer
"What is a gas grill?"

500 - extra outlet for Dad, education helper
"What is Dad's teaching at Moody?"

Best of Times

    100 - tree, tinsel, Grandma and Grandpa
      "What is Christmas?"
    200 - Grammy and Grandpa, reggae, "No problem, man!"
      "What is Jamaica?"
    300 - tape-recorded screams, candy, Bo in costume
      "What is Halloween?"
    400 - winter, wickets, kitchen utensils
      "What is indoor croquet?"
    500 - cars, cars, cars
      "What is the auto show?"

Use your own family's vacations, fun times, answers to prayer and projects (or any other ideas you might have) to compose your own game.

☐ With pencil or pen, write the *answers* on the corresponding squares on your game board. Be careful to write small enough so that your self-stick notes will cover the words in each square. Then, cover the answers with the self-stick notes. You may also want to write the point amount on the self-stick notes with a felt-tip pen.

☐ Write out the game rules. You may want to use this list:

a. Welcome to "Willifordy!" The object of this game is to give the correct corresponding question to the given answers. You will be attempting to give the correct questions for as many of these answers as you can.

b. The game will proceed in this manner: The youngest family member will choose the first square (any subject or point value). After I remove the self-stick note, the first person to ring the bell may attempt to answer correctly. If that person is *incorrect,* the next person to ring the bell may attempt an answer. If no one can answer correctly, no one receives the points. The family member giving the right answer may then choose the next square. (If no one answered correctly, then the youngest may then again choose the next square.) I will keep track of points awarded to each person. We will proceed in this manner until all the squares have been uncovered. (NOTE: You may want to play your version of the game by subtracting points for incorrect answers. We did not do this, to avoid too much of a competitive atmosphere.)

c. "Double Willifordy!" will then be played in this manner: Each family member will be given a 3″ x 5″ file card and a pencil. He or she must determine how much of his or her total points to risk on correctly answering this last question. After writing down an amount, the cards will be turned over and the "Double Willifordy!" question read aloud. Each person is to then record an answer on the file card. After a few minutes, I will ring the bell and read the correct answer. Points risked on an *incorrect* answer should be subtracted from that person's point total; points risked on a *correct* answer should be doubled and then added to that person's point total. The family member scoring the most points wins "Willifordy!"

☐ Pick a "Double Willifordy!" question. It should be a more challenging one. Write this and the answer on a file card.

☐ On a piano or keyboard, pick out the correct notes so that you can later play the familiar tune from the television game show. (This may sound difficult, but honestly, it's not! I was able to pick out the notes in only a few minutes.) Write down the music for later use.

☐ Set aside the game board, 3″ x 5″ file cards, pencils, notebook paper with answers and corresponding questions, bell, "Double Willifordy!" card, music, and keyboard for later.

FAMILY TIME:

1. Begin with prayer, thanking God for remembrances of fun times and answered prayers.

2. Announce cheerfully, "Welcome to 'Willifordy!' " and play the theme song. Bring out the game board, bell, and list of questions; read the game rules. Be sure to ask for any clarification of these rules. Proceed through the game and "Double Willifordy!" question, declaring a winner.

3. Close with a short prayer, again thanking God for what He has done for your family.

4. Fellowship over popcorn or a special treat, if desired.

SUGGESTIONS:

This family acitivity does demand a large commitment of time and creative energy on the planner's part. But please don't allow that to scare you away from attempting your own "Willifordy!" Instead, you may want to work at this over a time period of several weeks, accomplishing a step at a time. And I can truthfully say that this was one of those activities that I thoroughly enjoyed planning and putting together! (Can "Williford's 'Wheel of Pauperism' " be far behind?)

OLYMPICS

MATERIALS NEEDED:

☐ set of marbles (You will also need something to make a circle: chalk—if you're playing outside—or yarn or masking tape for inside.)

☐ battery-operated fish game in which players use small fishing rods to catch snapping fish

☐ Chinese checkers game with marbles

☐ tiddledywinks and target

☐ several empty wrapping paper tubes (one for each family member)

☐ watch with a second hand

☐ recorder (the instrument)

☐ family candle and matches

☐ baton (You may have a real one or substitute with ruler)

☐ poster board

☐ felt-tip pens (all colors)

☐ construction paper in various bright colors

☐ jar lid (for tracing circles)

☐ ribbon

☐ tape

☐ safety pins

☐ scissors

PREPARATION:

☐ Prepare the poster board which will list the games for your Olympics. At the top, you may wish to write out *"(your family's name)* Olympics" with a bright-colored felt-tip pen. Then, list the games in order of competition. The ones which we chose—and their corresponding family games—were these:

FISHING—the battery-operated fish game

*We played this game several times until the guys wanted to move on to the next competition.

SHARP SHOOTING—marbles

*Using a piece of yarn on our indoor-outdoor carpet in the family room, we played marbles.

SWIMMING — recorder
*As I explained to my family, championship swimmers have excellent lungs. Therefore, the family member who could blow on the recorder for the longest amount of time proved he or she had the strongest lungs

SUMO WRESTLING — Chinese Checkers
*I realize that sumo wrestling involves *Japanese* wrestlers, so we renamed this game Chinese/Japanese Checkers!

ARCHERY — tiddledywinks
*Shooting and aiming for the targets with tiddledywinks was our version of archery.

SWORD PLAY — bonker fight
*Bonker battles with empty wrapping paper tubes are *always* a favorite with my family!

RELAY RACES — passing the baton for sharing
*As we sat around the table containing our lighted family candle, we passed the "baton" and shared a favorite memory from the past year.

If you do not have some of these supplies, you may want to decide on your own creative ideas for games. Also, if your children currently have games in which they are very interested (such as jacks, jump rope, video games or badminton), incorporate these into your list.

Whatever games you eventually decide to use, list these on the poster board in a colorful and eye-catching way. I drew a small picture next to each major sport also. (NOTE: You may want to leave out the words "marbles," "Chinese checkers," etc., as I did; this way the actual activity will be a surprise.)

☐ Collect and assemble all materials necessary for the games.

☐ Make ribbons to award to winners. First, cut out circles from many different colors of construction paper by tracing around jar lids. Make several cuts toward the center of these circles, bending these tabs slightly, to create a decorated effect. With felt-tip pens, write *Winner! Congratulations!* or draw happy faces on the circles. Lastly, tape cut ribbons onto the backs of the circles. (NOTE: I would avoid labeling these "first place" or "second place" in an attempt to avoid too much competition. This way you can award ribbons to those winning the game—and those who may have come in last but "played a terrific game.")

☐ Set aside game supplies, candle and matches, poster board and ribbons, and safety pins for later.

FAMILY TIME:

1. Begin with prayer, thanking God for games which exercise our bodies, minds, and family fellowship.

2. Announce that you will be having the *"(Your family's name) Olympics"*—right here, tonight! Holding up the poster board, point out the individual games that all of you will be competing in. Announce that award ribbons will be given for winners *and* good sports.

3. Proceed through each game, spending as much time on each one as family members seem to desire. (HINT: Boredom, arguing, or "perpetual giggle stage" means move on to the next game.)

4. For the relay game, gather around your table. After lighting the family candle and turning the lights down low, explain that you will pass the "baton" to one another, taking turns sharing a favorite memory from the past year. (Or, you may decide on another topic on which you would like your family to share.) You may pass the baton as many times as you wish.

5. End with family prayer.

SUGGESTIONS:

When I showed my family the list of games which we would be playing, all three looked at me with amused and puzzled expressions. They knew we certainly wouldn't be fishing, sharp shooting, swimming, wrestling (and definitely not *sumo* style!), shooting arrows, fighting with swords, or running relay races—and so they all knew Mom was up to some creative ideas again!

Any time I can arouse my family's curiosity, keep their interest, and excite them with fun games, I judge I have accomplished much. The "Williford Olympics" met all three objectives—and then ended with a warm sharing time of fellowship!

As my sons continue to grow and change, slowly (or is it quickly—much too quickly?) becoming more *men* than *boys,* I constantly find myself wondering, "What will they truly be like when they are adults? Will these devotions have made a difference in their lives, causing them to know God better and therefore transform into the Christlikeness that Craig and I so desire for them?"

Obviously, I can't and don't know the answers to these concerns; they remain part of the unknown *future.* But the desire to provide an atmosphere and vehicle for my sons' spiritual growth is one I must address in the *now.* I am responsible for the *now.* I can work to invest in the *now.* And thus, week after week, year after year, this family continues to commit to family worship.

Yes, this takes work, time, and energy. It means we must say no to other worthwhile activities. And we still don't know what the future holds for our beloved sons. But Craig and I do know we won't be tortured with questions of *"Why didn't we. . . . ?"* concerning commitment to a night for family worship.

Will you?

Commentaries

Leon Morris, ed., *Tyndale New Testament Commentaries* (multiple volumes) (Grand Rapids, Mich.: Eerdmans Publishing Co.).

John F. Walvoord and Roy B. Zuck, eds., *The Bible Knowledge Commentary,* New Testament (Wheaton, Ill.: Victor Books, 1983).

John F. Walvoord and Roy B. Zuck, eds., *The Bible Knowledge Commentary,* Old Testament (Wheaton, Ill.: Victor Books, 1985).

D.J. Wiseman, ed., *Tyndale Old Testament Commentaries* (multiple volumes) (Downers Grove, Ill.: InterVarsity Press).

Introductions

Norman L. Geisler, *A Popular Survey of the Old Testament* (Grand Rapids, Mich.: Baker Book House, 1977).

Robert H. Gundry, *A Survey of the New Testament,* rev. ed. (Grand Rapids, Mich.: Zondervan Publishing House, 1981).

Concordances

Orville J. Nave, *Nave's Topical Bible* (Chicago, Ill.: Moody Press, 1974).

James Strong, *The Exhaustive Concordance of the Bible* (Nashville, Tenn.: Abingdon, 1978).

Background Encyclopedias

V. Gilbert Beers, *The Victor Handbook of Bible Knowledge* (Wheaton, Ill.: Victor Books, 1981).

Merrill C. Tenney, ed., *The Zondervan Pictorial Encyclopedia of the Bible* (five volumes) (Grand Rapids, Mich.: Zondervan Publishing House, 1975).

Fred H. Wright, *Manners and Customs of Bible Lands* (Chicago, Ill.: Moody Press, 1953).

The Illustrated Bible Dictionary (four volumes) (Wheaton, Ill.: Tyndale House Publishers, 1980).

Bibles

Kenneth Barker, ed., *The NIV Study Bible* (Grand Rapids, Mich.: Zondervan Bible Publishers, 1985).

The New International Version Young Discoverer's Bible (Grand Rapids, Mich.: Zondervan Bible Publishers, 1985).

Fiction

Paula Fox, *One-Eyed Cat* (New York: Bradbury Press, 1984).

Ken Gire, Jr., *The Christmas Duck* (Milford, Mich.: Mott Media, Inc., 1983).

Madeleine L'Engle, *A Wrinkle in Time* (This is followed by *A Wind in the Door* and *A Swiftly Tilting Planet.)* (New York: Dell Pub. Co., Inc., 1976).

C.S. Lewis, *The Lion, the Witch and the Wardrobe* (This is book one in *The Chronicles of Narnia;* there are seven in this series.) (New York: Macmillan Pub. Co., 1950).

David and Karen Mains, *Tales of the Kingdom* (Elgin, Ill.: David C. Cook Pub. Co., 1983).

David and Karen Mains, *Tales of the Resistance* (Elgin, Ill.: David C. Cook Pub. Co., 1986).

Janette Oke, *Love Comes Softly* (There are eight in this series.) (Minneapolis, Minn.: Bethany House Pub., 1979).

Janette Oke, *When Calls the Heart* (There are four in this series.) (Minneapolis, Minn.: Bethany House Pub., 1983).

Resources for Teens

James Dobson, *Preparing for Adolescence* (Ventura, Calif.: Regal Books, 1978).

James Dobson, *Preparing for Adolescence: Growth Guide* (Ventura, Calif.: Regal Books, 1979).

TITLE INDEX